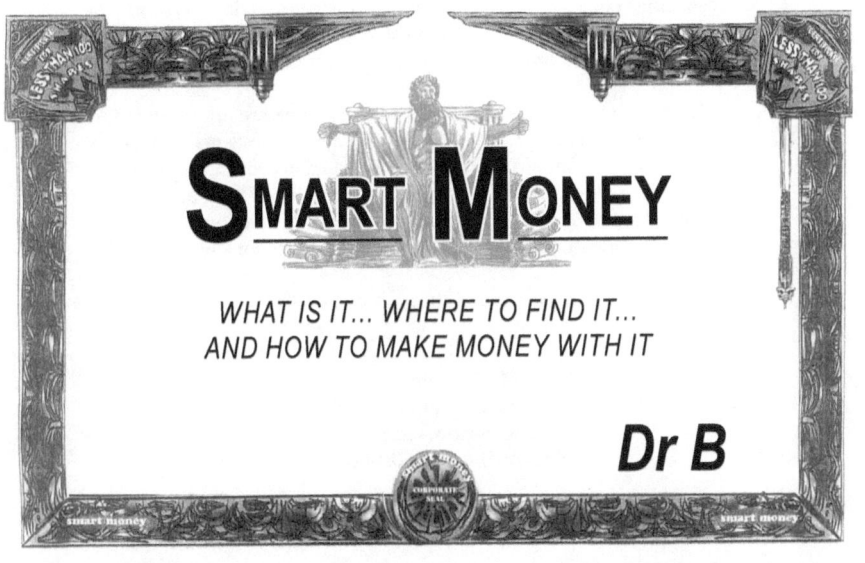

SMART MONEY

WHAT IS IT... WHERE TO FIND IT...
AND HOW TO MAKE MONEY WITH IT

Dr B

iUniverse, Inc.
Bloomington

Smart Money
What Is It... Where To Find It...
And How To Make Money With It

Copyright © 2012 William Baumner

All rights reserved. No part of this book may be used or reproduced by any means, graphic, electronic, or mechanical, including photocopying, recording, taping or by any information storage retrieval system without the written permission of the publisher except in the case of brief quotations embodied in critical articles and reviews.

The information, ideas, and suggestions in this book are not intended to render professional advice. Before following any suggestions contained in this book, you should consult your personal accountant or other financial advisor. Neither the author nor the publisher shall be liable or responsible for any loss or damage allegedly arising as a consequence of your use or application of any information or suggestions in this book.

iUniverse books may be ordered through booksellers or by contacting:

iUniverse
1663 Liberty Drive
Bloomington, IN 47403
www.iuniverse.com
1-800-Authors (1-800-288-4677)

Because of the dynamic nature of the Internet, any Web addresses or links contained in this book may have changed since publication and may no longer be valid. The views expressed in this work are solely those of the author and do not necessarily reflect the views of the publisher, and the publisher hereby disclaims any responsibility for them.

Any people depicted in stock imagery provided by Thinkstock are models, and such images are being used for illustrative purposes only.

Certain stock imagery © Thinkstock.

ISBN: 978-1-4759-1150-3 (sc)
ISBN: 978-1-4759-1151-0 (hc)
ISBN: 978-1-4759-1152-7 (e)

Library of Congress Control Number: 2012908345

Printed in the United States of America

iUniverse rev. date: 11/28/2012

To all of us who have lost money in the financial markets honestly.

Foreword

I wish that there had been a book like this somewhere during my studies in school or during my early years as a stockbroker. Then again, if there had been a book with this information, I would have probably been retired, and so maybe would you. And then there wouldn't be a need for this book.

Nonetheless, I owe a lot to a number of people that have influenced me over the past twenty-five years. I gleaned a tremendous amount of information from them that ultimately led me to write this book. I was fortunate enough to have had the pleasure of meeting many successful traders, analysts, brokers, financial advisors, and money managers. I believe that we all can learn something from everyone we come in contact with.

The market is very unforgiving, and no one has the Holy Grail for making money in the market on a continuous basis. However, we think that our philosophy and strategy will have a great impact—not only on how you invest, but also how you think. The research, ideas, and information come from the work of PhDs in mathematics and finance. We have spent the greater part of our lifetimes gathering the information. Remember that the quotes you will read are from some very credible, knowledgeable people.

I thank everyone for their thoughts, advice, and input over the years. I just wish that this book had been written years earlier.

When you follow the **smart money**, you will do two things. First, you will dramatically increase your chances for making money. Perhaps even more important is how you apply this philosophy to how you live and make decisions in this rapidly changing world. You will not get easily taken or misled as so many people have. You will understand how important it is to find accurate information and why that information is not going to be so common or easily found. It will take some initiative on your part and require some legwork. However, it will help you and might just change your life as it has mine.

If you understand the philosophies and employ the strategies in this book, you will look at the world differently and invest differently. However, I hope that this information impacts your life and your net worth in a positive manner—as it has mine.

Contents

Introduction 1
What Is Smart Money? 5
Insider Trading 9
Who Controls the Markets? 23
Historical Perspective 47
Where It Really All Started 51
The 2008 Economic Crisis 59
The Financial Market Meltdown 65
What Causes Bubbles to Burst? 75
What Drives the Stock Market? 79
Why Follow Smart Money? 83
How Smart Money Works 93
Not All Insiders Are Equal 99
What Forms Insiders Use 103
Insiders at Work 105
9/11 and the Options Market 115
The Largest Insider Trading Scam Ever . . .119
Where to Find the Information 123
Where Is the Smart Money Today? 127
Conclusion 131
Index 139

Introduction

As I stated in the foreword, I wish that there had been a book like this for all of us investors. At one time, I had four or five different brokers. I thought that surely one could help me make some good money. Nope. I guess I was just too small a client to have a broker that was that good or connected.

I had a couple of mutual funds that my father had started for me as a child, which seemed to have performed nicely. One of which was Peter Lynch's Fidelity Magellan Fund, which did very well while he was there. I was a shareholder for three or four years. The fund was doing well, and then he decided to retire. As soon as he left, so did the returns. Just my luck.

I thought that I would become a broker and find the secret way to consistently make money in the markets. Maybe through sheer experience I would find a way to increase the potential rate of return for my clients as a broker and for my own portfolio. Nope—that didn't work either, so I thought that education would provide me with the answers. I studied enough to get the degrees that I thought would provide me with the answers. That didn't work. I combed through periodical after periodical, reading all the financial literature I could get my hands on, looking for the Holy Grail of investing. Still nothing.

It took me many years to finally realize that there is no Holy Grail to investing. There is no foolproof trading software, technique, or strategy that will provide consistent returns. There are many knowledgeable, smart people in the financial industry. But it just didn't seem to matter who I listened to or followed.

However, I knew that there were many people increasing their net worth each and every year. Just read the *Forbes* magazine's wealthiest families edition every year. You will see a lot of the same names year after year, despite whether the stock market, real estate market, or whatever market crashed or performed terribly that year. I wondered how that was possible.

I try to read all of the research published by research firms. I read all of the so-called newsletter gurus. Sometimes I would find something that worked, but not very often. I follow people that are considered experts by the financial media. Still very disappointing. I visit the money shows, visit literally hundreds of seminars. And still nothing. I figured that I must find those extremely well-educated money managers and analysts that get paid very well for their insight. It is tough to do—and it's hit or miss at best.

I cannot begin to tell you how many hundreds of thousands of dollars that I have lost by listening to others, following other people's well-intentioned recommendations. I know that there probably have been billions of dollars lost by millions of investors, which is why this book is even more important.

The insight and information in this book will not only change how you invest, but also how you understand, relate to, and look at the rest of the world. This will be one of the most important books you may ever read.

This book is written for everyone. It is simple in terms and strategy. You do not need a PhD in finance to understand and profit from this book. I have written this book in easy to understand language, almost as if we are just having a normal conversation, so that anyone can understand and learn from this writing. In fact, when you are done reading this, you will have more knowledge about how to make money and how things work than any finance-degree program ever teaches. And you will know more about how the financial markets operate than probably 99 percent of the general public.

You will receive an education in how to be smart with your money when it comes to investing that you will not get from financial magazines, newspapers, or books. If you only read one finance book in your lifetime, this is the one. This is the only one you need to understand how the ***smart money*** in this country—and around the world—operates, and how you need to invest if you want to make money. Period.

What Is Smart Money?

We have identified through extensive and exhaustive research that *smart money* is not only big money, but it is also quiet money. *Smart money* truly is *smart money*. As strange as that may sound, it is not just big money, but it is quiet money also.

Now there is a difference between big money and *smart money*. And it's vitally important that you understand and recognize the difference.

Some say that the big money in the nineties was in mutual funds that were buying large cap growth and technology stocks. For nearly a decade, the big money was the *smart money*. But when the tech bubble burst, the big money got crushed and became risk averse. Meanwhile in 2003–2004—when the markets began to show signs of rebound—the *smart money* was buying oil, metals, Real Estate Investment Trusts (REITs), commodities, and emerging markets.

But you don't want to confuse big money with piles of money from the masses. Yes, you can make money in the short term by following the big money or "herd" mentality—what Wall Street calls "momentum investing." However, as you probably already know, you can get hurt—and hurt badly.

Therefore, our definition of big money is typically very large individual investors or very large pools of money managed by well-connected or "in-the-know" people. You will be able to clearly discern **smart money** from big money after reading this book. We have provided numerous examples for you to learn from and use to profit from in the future.

We have noticed over the years that the ultra-wealthy and people "in-the-know" seem to somehow increase their net worth every year, despite how bad the stock, bond, gold, commodity, or real estate markets do. How do they do it? We all have access to the same research, don't we? We all have access to the Internet and can access ideas, research, opinions, reports, and recommendations.

This is sort of true, but herein lies the key. The general public and the investing masses tend to act and behave like sheep; they tend to get led astray. And we all know that sheep tend to get slaughtered. How can we avoid getting slaughtered?

First you have to think outside the box, drink upstream from the herd, and zig when the masses are zagging. Short of obtaining inside information, this is the only way. We are not legally able to trade on non-public information. This is what the Securities and Exchange Commission (SEC) calls "insider trading," which is illegal.

Now this type of trading unfortunately still takes place. That's right. Just notice the volume in the stock options or in the stock itself a day or two before a big announcement or buyout occurs. This is not supposed to happen, but it does. What happens when you see big volume in a stock to the upside or downside, but there is no news? Somebody knows something; they are buying or selling to reflect that information or knowledge. Pay particular attention to these situations.

In a following chapter, you will read about the largest insider trading scam in United States history, which very few people know about.

However, this is not what this book is about and we certainly do not recommend anything that is illegal, unethical, or immoral. It is not worth going to jail over a few dollars. The chances are pretty good that you will get caught with today's high-tech surveillance and technology available to the SEC. Don't worry. You can make money ethically. If you are super-well-connected, then you probably have everything you need and want. But for most of us, this book is a necessity.

How do they do it? Some get lucky, but you can't be lucky all the time. No, they do it because they have something that you and I do not have: accurate and timely information. Pure and simple.

Insider Trading

We are going to spend some significant time in this book to a subject that is both misunderstood and not understood at all by most investors. It is a very important topic which you need to fully understand along with its potential implications. We are not legally able to trade on inside information or material non–public information. This is what the Securities and Exchange Commission (SEC) calls "insider trading", which is illegal.

Insider trading has been banned in the US for more than forty years. Unfortunately though, this type of trading still takes place. That's right. If you don't believe me, that is ok. You will see from the following pages just how much this occurs and is a serious problem. In fact, it takes place more frequently than we are led to believe and more than the regulatory bodies and media tell us. Soon you will read about the largest insider trading scam in world history that took place in 2008, which never made any headlines in the mass media or financial media for that matter. Nor were there any SEC investigations into the trading that took place. Utterly incredible, and unbelievable, as you will soon read.

In fact, here is an example of what I am talking about that relates directly to the stock market. On Thursday, August 4, 2011, the Dow Jones dropped over 500 points. We all wondered why such a bad day, because we didn't see any news to account for the massive drop. It turns out the very next day, after the market closed mind you, that Standard & Poor's (S&P) came out and downgraded the debt of the US. Imagine that! This is precisely what I mean. Obviously someone or someone's knew about this and traded on this information. Is this fair, is this right? Of course not!

But there is a lot more to this that you need to be aware of. First, Dean Baker, co-director of the Center for Economic and Policy Research, said "The Treasury Department revealed that S&P's decision was initially based on a $2 trillion error in accounting. However, even after this enormous error was corrected, S&P went ahead with the downgrade." This would suggest that they made the decision to downgrade despite the evidence to the contrary. Hmmmmm…I wonder why.

Paul Krugman in the New York Times stated "Everything I've heard about S&P's demands suggests that it's talking nonsense about the US fiscal situation. The agency has suggested that the downgrade depended on the size of agreed deficit reduction over the next decade, with $4 trillion apparently the magic number. Yet US solvency depends hardly at all on what happens in the near or even medium term; an extra trillion in debt adds only a fraction of a percent of GDP to future interest costs. In short, S&P is just making stuff up- and after the mortgage debacle, they really don't have that right."

Jason Schwarz wrote in an article Seeking Alpha titled "The Rise of Financial Terrorism", "After the market close on Friday, August 5th, we received word that S&P CEO Deven Sharma had taken control of the ratings agency and personally led the push for a US downgrade. There is a lot of evidence that he has deliberately tried to trash the US economy. Even after discovering that the S&P debt calculations were off by $2 trillion, Sharma made the decision to go ahead with the unethical downgrade. This is a guy who was a key contributor at the 2009 Bilderberger Summit that organized 120 of the world's richest men and women to push for an end to the dollar as the global reserve currency."

Come to find out, Sharma has stated in writing that he considers the US the problem in today's world, operating with what he implies is an unfair and reckless advantage. The brutal reality is that for globalization to succeed the US must be torn asunder.

Are you kidding me? And this guy was the CEO of the largest and most prestigious and influential of all the US ratings agencies?

Schwarz also stated that Michael Barnier, head of European Regulation is another suspect in market manipulations. He blocked the plan of Hans Hoogervorst, the newly appointed Chairman of the International Accounting Standards Board, to save Europe by adopting a new rule called IFRS 9. The rule would have eliminated mark to market accounting of sovereign debt from European bank balance sheets.

The dangers of mark to market accounting are well known as evidenced by the US's recent banking crisis in 2008-2009, and the 1930's Depression. Mark to market accounting was repealed on April 2, 2009, which finally put an end to the liquidity crisis, and contributed to a recovery in the stock market. US banks no longer had to raise capital as the financial markets regained stability. The exact same scenario would have happened like this in 2011 in Europe under Hoogervorst's plan.

It's interesting to note that Barnier, like Sharma, was a confirmed attendee at past Bilderberger conferences. What are the Bilderberger's and why mention them here? According to Daniel Estulin, noted expert on the Bilderbergers, describes that secretive globalist group as "a medium of bringing together financial institutions which are the world's most powerful and most predatory financial interests."

In June 2011, he stated, Bilderberg isn't a secret society... It's a meeting of people who represent a certain ideology...Not One World Government or New World Order as too many people mistakenly believe. Rather the ideology is of a One World Company Limited. The 'world company" was a term used at a Bilderberger meeting in Canada in 1968 by the US Undersecretary of State for Economic Affairs and a managing director of banking giants Lehman Brothers and Kuhn Loeb.

Estulin goes on: The idea behind each and every Bilderberg meeting is to create what they themselves call THE ARISTOCRACY OF PURPOSE between European and North American elites on the best way to manage the planet. In other words, the creation of a global network of giant cartels, more powerful than any nation on Earth, destined to control the necessities of life of the rest of humanity."

Understand that the world company acquires assets by preventing governments from issuing their own currencies and credit. Money is created by banks as loans of interest. The debts grow and grow, until more is owed than created in the original loans. If currencies are not allowed to expand to meet increased costs and growth, then a wave of bankruptcies, foreclosures, and sales of assets at firesale prices. Sales to whom? To the world company.

We are grateful to the Washington Post, The New York Times, Time magazine and other great publications whose directors

> *have attended our meetings and respected their promises of discretion for almost forty years…It would have been impossible for us to develop our plan for the world if we had been subjected to the lights of publicity during those years. But, the world is now more sophisticated and prepared to march towards a world government. The supranational sovereignty of an intellectual elite and world bankers is surely preferable to the national autodetermination practiced in past centuries.*
> —David Rockefeller (at the Bilderberg meeting in 1991)

A week after the US debt downgrade, the SEC asked S&P to disclose which employees knew of its decision to downgrade the US debt before it was announced. And get this, the very next week, the president of S&P Deven Sharma resigned! Hello? Am I the only one that thinks something smells here? I mean come on, this is pathetic. Yet you don't hear anyone questioning anybody about this in the financial or mainstream media. I wonder why!?! The facts remain that the market action in early August was unprecedented, unnatural, and certainly warrants an investigation.

We devote time and attention to the S&P downgrade of the US debt, not just because of how the market traded, but the fact that someone made a very large bet on July 21 with trades of 5,370 ten year Treasury futures and 3,100 Treasury bond futures, according to ETF Daily News. Someone made 1,000 per cent return on their money, all in two weeks or close to $10 billion! This person made this huge bet with the expectation that interest rates would go up after the S&P issued a credit downgrade. US Treasury Secretary Timothy Geithner said in April that there was no risk of a downgrade. So, someone knew something in order to make such a huge bet before the rest of us knew anything. How many of you reading this right now ever heard about this? This is why this strategy is so important because if we had all followed this trade, we all could have made substantial gains. I mean when was the last time you made 1000 percent on your money in two weeks?!

One of the wealthiest men in the world is billionaire George Soros. He is a man that has been convicted for insider trading in France and fined US$2.9 million dollars and fined US$ 2.5 million dollars for illegal market manipulation in Hungary.

In April 2011, the Securities and Exchange Commission alleged $32 million worth of insider trading on 11 merger deals by a corporate lawyer and trader Matthew H. Kluger and Garrett D. Bauer. Apparently, they communicated through a middle man to execute the trades and were later arrested, according to a SEC release on April 6, 2011.

And on September 21, 2011, Reuters reported that a former Goldman Sachs employee and his father were charged by US regulators with insider trading related to confidential information about trading strategies for exchange traded funds (ETF's).

The commission said that NY resident Spencer Mindlin, 33, was able to get nonpublic information about Goldman's plans to buy and sell securities underlying the SPDR S&P Retail Exchange Traded Fund (XRT). The SEC said that Spencer then tipped off his father, 68, a certified public accountant. Together, the SEC alleges, that the two traded illegally in four different securities that underlie the ETF.

The insider trading allegedly took place between December 2007 and March 2008. Goldman Sachs was the largest institutional holder of XRT so that its customers could short it. Goldman also shorted the various securities underlying the ETF in order to hedge its long position.

The complaint alleges that the two men made at least $57,000 in illicit trading profits.

Now your probably wondering why is the SEC frying such a small fish when there are sharks and whales out there. True, good point. But just realize that insider trading can occur not just in stocks, but bonds, ETF's, and basically anything that trades, whether it is public or private, liquid or illiquid.

Look at the options market as well. Pay particular attention to sharp dramatic increases in the volume in the options market for individual stocks or in the individual stock a day or two before a big announcement like earnings or a buyout occurs. Volume typically precedes price. You might find a stock that will trade five, ten, maybe even twenty times its average daily volume and there is no news. Why do you suppose the volume? Someone knows something. You will notice the stock will make a dramatic move shortly thereafter, and news will follow. You think all these people got lucky? Maybe a few did, but not all of them. Don't be naïve. Look at the stock charts to see huge volume increases and notice how the stock moves shortly thereafter, and then check to see when news came out. That's right. This is not supposed to happen, but it does. Whenever you see big volume in a stock to the upside or downside, and there is no news? Well, somebody somewhere knows something, and is buying or selling to reflect that information or knowledge.

So pay particular attention to these situations. As I stated earlier, usually volume precedes price. And when you see stocks trade five, ten or whatever large number times their average thirty day or 6 month volume and there is no news…Hello? What do you think is going on? Pay attention. I cannot tell you how many times I would find a stock trading with huge, abnormal, unusual volume and there was no news to be found anywhere.

And I wonder, does anyone else notice, because this happens more frequently then you may think. Of course, shortly after the volume spike, news comes out and the stock trades higher or lower. Sometimes it is a buy or sell recommendation from a major brokerage firm, earnings, a buyout or something important to create investor appetite and interest. There are people, investors, traders, and money managers that do nothing but watch where the big unusual volume is in stocks each day, and then invest accordingly. The point is, that insider trading still takes place here in the US and it is a huge problem for regulators.

Just take a look at the hedge fund billionaire Raj Rajaratnam who was convicted of 14 counts of insider trading in May 2011. Here is a guy that coaxed corporate insiders into giving him an illegal edge or material non public information with which he used to make huge sums of money. This was the largest insider trading case ever involving hedge funds.

It turns out that Raj was guilty of insider trading on stocks including Google and Goldman Sachs. Why is it that no one from Goldman Sachs is charged with providing non-public information to Raj?

Berkshire Hathaway directors accused David Sokol, once considered the man to succeed Warren Buffett, of misleading the company about his huge personal stake in Lubrizol that Berkshire agreed to acquire in the first quarter of 2011. Mr. Sokol, who resigned in March, never told Warren Buffett that he had bought a stake in Lubrizol after Citigroup bankers pitched the company as a potential takeover target. So then you are probably wondering why does one man go to jail for insider trading and the other get to take millions in cash and retire? How is this fair? It is important to ask these questions, but even more important to understand why this occurs. It turns out Buffett is one of the largest individual shareholders of Goldman Sachs. You will learn more about who Goldman Sachs is later.

In late October 2011, Rajat Gupta surrendered to the FBI to face charges of insider trading. Here is a guy that graduated from Harvard, and was the CEO of McKinsey and Company which encouraged Enron's transformation from a quiet energy pipeline company into a high-risk trading operation that ultimately filed bankruptcy protection amid a huge accounting scandal. And if that wasn't enough, Gupta was a former director at Goldman Sachs.

In a subsequent following chapter, you will read about the largest insider trading scam in US history, of which very few people even know about. It was never widely publicized in the media for a number of reasons, which you will understand as you examine what took place in the financial markets. An absolute travesty of epic proportion.

However, this is not what this book is about and we certainly do not recommend anything that is illegal, unethical or immoral. The chances are pretty good that you can and will get caught today with all the high tech surveillance and technology available to the regulators. You should also know that the Consumer Financial Protection Bureau was just created to help oversee the financial industry which will employ more than twice the number of people that the SEC currently employs. Don't worry. You can make money ethically.

Now, if you just so happen to be a genius or you are a visionary when it comes to investing, then you don't need this book. Please pass it on to someone who isn't. If you are super well connected, then you probably have everything you need and want. For most of us, this book is a necessity.

So then how do these super well connected or smart people

do it? Sure some get lucky, but you can't be lucky all the time. No, they do it because they have two things that you and I do not have. Those two things are **accurate** and **timely information**. Pure and simple.

Now for the real deal on Insider Trading. ***Perhaps the most telling, revealing, relevant, incredible, pertinent information in this book***. And again, most people have no clue that this takes place and is allowed. Get yourself real comfortable, because what you are about to read is as I said earlier, almost unbelievable. However, in light of what has been going on in Washington, maybe it is not so shocking.

We all know that politicians in Washington that serve in Congress have incredible jobs, what with all the ancillary benefits, medical insurance, and retirement benefits that they receive. In fact, arguably one of if not the best jobs in the world. However, and here it comes. Did you know that our politicians can make as much money as they want on insider trading? Lawmakers and their staffers are specifically exempted. This means that members of the House and Senate who might be working on or studying pending legislation and regulatory changes can trade on that non-public material information and make as much money as they want.

Valerie Richardson at the Washington Times, stated "Strict laws ban corporate executives from trading on their insider knowledge, but no restrictions exist for members of Congress. Lawmakers are permitted to keep their holdings and trade shares on the market, as well as vote on legislation that could affect their portfolio values."

How significant is this? Well, there have been a number of significant studies on this. One such study showed that the common stock portfolios of United States Senators beat the market by 12% a year, on average between 1993 and 1998, according to a study by economist Alan Ziobrowski and his team.[1]

Another more recent study came from a number of academicians from different universities in the US. Here is what they discovered. Examinations covering 16,000 common stock transactions made by approximately 300 House representatives from 1985-2001, and found what they termed "significant positive abnormal returns." Imagine that. In fact, the congressional trades beat the market by about 6.6% annually.[2]

What's their secret? The report postulates but does not conclude that it might have something to do with the ability members of Congress have to trade on material, non-public information and maybe to vote their own pocketbooks.

Another study by the same academicians found in 2006 that members of the Senate beat the market by about 10 percent annually, an amount the academicians stated was "both economically large and statistically significant."

In 2008, just one month before oil prices took a massive plunge, Senator Harry Reid sold between $15,000 and $50,000 of stocks in the oil industry that he owned in the Dow Jones Energy Index. Coincidence, or maybe just luck?? Hold on for a minute. Soon thereafter, Reid then purchased between $15,000 and $50,000 worth of healthcare holdings in the Dow Jones Health Care Index at a time when he was contemplating rewriting healthcare laws.[3]

According to the ReviewJournal.com on Oct 11, 2010, a senior energy aide nearly doubled his money in five months by

---

[1] Jane j. Kim, US senators' Stock Picks outperform the Pro's, Wall St. J., Oct 26, 2004.
[2] Abnormal Returns From The Common Stock Investments of Members of the US House of Representatives.
[3] http://finance.townhall.com

buying and selling an energy company at a time when Congress was considering an industry tax break.

Perhaps what really put the spotlight on all this was the Sunday, November 13, 2011 airing of CBS's 60 Minutes which revealed former House Speaker Nancy Pelosi and her hefty returns from her stock picks. The Pelosi's bought 5,000 shares of Visa at the initial public offering price of $44. Turns out there was legislation that would have hurt credit card companies making its way through the House. However, it never actually made it to the floor of the House. Two days later Visa was at $64. A $100,000 profit in 2 days.

The point is that there are numerous examples that you can find showing how members of Congress, staff and aides have made money based on information that they were privy to.[4]

"In the course of performing their normal duties, members of Congress have access to non-public information that could have a substantial impact on certain businesses, industries or the economy as a whole. If used as the basis for common stock transactions, such information could yield significant personal trading profits, the researchers stated.[5]

This may not sound like much, but if you outperform the market by 6% on average for a number of years, the money starts to add up rather significantly. They say that as many as 90% of all mutual funds and money managers underperform the market every year. Thus for one to not only beat the market every year but by 1200 basis points or 12% is significant in the investment world.

The SEC has been unwilling to enforce insider trading by members of Congress, their aides, and staffers. So it appears as

---

4 ReviewJournal.com, Washington Bureau, October 11, 2010.
5 Abnormal Returns From The Common Stock Investments of Members of the US House of Representatives.

though it will continue, despite the Congressional ethics rules. There is no limit to just how much money one can earn on insider trading in the House or Senate.

The point here is that unless you are a member of Congress, you can't legally invest your money based on inside information or material, non-public information. Insider trading is illegal for us, which means that you need this book.

And wouldn't you know, just as this book is going to press, on February 2, 2012, the Senate approved an insider trading bill. It isn't as strong as it should have been. Although, I guess something is better than nothing. What this bill seeks to do is prohibit lawmakers and their families from buying and selling securities based on their knowledge of non-public information. It requires lawmakers to report transactions within 30 days of buying and selling. These trades also have to be published in a searchable, online database.

Now, just remember that corporate insider trading rules require reporting of trades within two business days instead of the 30 days that Congress and lawmakers now have. This means that there will be many times that by the time you see trades from Congress, the security may have already made a substantial move. In the case where they haven't, pay particular attention.

It is so important in today's financial world that investors find an accurate, time proven methodology that can potentially increase the rate of return on investments. We are all looking for an "edge", a way to beat the market. There are so many people that claim big returns, and the next great super stock" but in actuality, all they are doing is selling you and I a bill of goods. And I have a lot of goods. So many goods that they compile a number of book cases that truly are not worth their own weight in dollars or gold. Well, then again maybe in dollars. Although, what our government is doing to our dollar might someday soon be worth exactly what all these goods are really worth…nothing!

Our world is changing, but more importantly our financial landscape. The central banks and governments around the world are influencing our lives in ways that many of us thought would never happen. Our lives are being impacted and changed right before our very eyes in ways that many of us are totally oblivious to. And quite honestly, I am not sure that most Americans even care. But for those of us that do, read on.

WHO CONTROLS THE MARKETS?

One of the most important things that you must recognize—but not necessarily understand—is that all markets are controlled and/or manipulated. Before you decide that this is the most absurd or ludicrous thing you ever heard of, read on.

We do not care what market you want to invest in. All markets are heavily influenced or controlled. It doesn't matter whether one is talking about oil (largely controlled by OPEC), diamonds (largely controlled by DeBeers), or gold.

Twice per day, representatives of four major London banking firms (Mocatta & Goldsmid, Samuel Montagu & Co., Sharps Pixley, and Johnson Matheson) meet in the offices of N M Rothschild Co. in London to fix the price of gold. Really? How many analysts—and so-called gold experts—share that with you? How many people actually know this? Well, it's time you do.

As I add the finishing touches to this book, a US Senate panel will vote on legislation designed to allow the US Department of Justice to sue OPEC for gasoline price-fixing. Give me a break. You think this will actually work? A similar bill passed the House in 2008 by a close vote of 324-84!, enough to override a presidential veto, but still never made it into law. If the Federal Reserve were to raise interest rates and the US government were to stop spending money, gasoline prices would fall. They could at least start with lowering the federal tax of .244 cents per gallon on diesel fuel if they wanted. Federal and state taxes essentially mean that the US government nets a bigger chunk of gasoline profits than oil companies. When was the last time you heard that in the mass media?

In smaller markets, manipulation of prices is much easier. That's right. Take for example the natural gas futures markets. In April 2011, the Federal Energy Regulatory Commission (FERC) fined former Amaranth Advisors' lead energy trader Brian Hunter $30 million in a civil penalty for violating the Commission's anti-manipulation rules in the natural gas futures market and concluded that "this amount is appropriate and sufficient to discourage Hunter and others from engaging in market manipulation." Really? You really think so?

In April 2011, oil traded over $112 per barrel for light Texas sweet crude. The mass media reported that the price of oil was going up because of speculators. Apparently, President Obama did not agree with the message sent by FERC regarding manipulation of the energy markets, by announcing that his administration has created a financial task force to look into the manipulation in the oil markets specifically. Come on now, really?

And why does the government repeatedly point to speculators as to the reason we have high prices? Do you really think that if somehow we limited speculating in oil that somehow the price would be lower? Look at what is happening to commodities that do not even trade on exchanges. If people would just wake up and realize this line of thinking is totally ridiculous, then maybe things would change. I mean if speculators always make prices go higher, please shift them into the housing market. There are speculators betting that prices will go higher and lower in just about everything. What does have a far greater effect on the price of oil are the monetary and fiscal policies which directly affect the US dollar. You can also include the impact that taxes and massive regulations have had. Proof that this is true is that you will not see anything turn up from the investigation regarding speculators of any market moving significance.

After the financial crash of 2008-2009, there has not been one indictment of a Wall Street executive regarding the massive speculative bubble that destroyed the housing market and economy. Imagine that! And what about the speculators that supposedly caused the internet and technology bubble of 2000?

Just know that markets can be influenced by speculators. No doubt about it. But it's who or what that controls the markets that counts.

Take cocoa for example. In the spring of 2011, cocoa hit its highest price in 32 years. It did so not because of a shortage of cocoa or unusual heavy demand for chocolate. It was up largely due to the fact that the Ivory Coast's asserting control over its supply, some 40% of world production, according to Reuters.

I think you get the idea now. You can do your own research and find out who the real players are in whatever market you are involved in as an investor. You may have to make a couple of phone calls to speak to a number of different traders in whatever market you are interested in to get their insight, but it might just save you some money. You have to know who makes the rules, if you want to play in their game or in other words invest in their market.

CNN Money in late April 2011 reported that "High oil prices are here to stay and they're caused by surging demand and limited new supply, not Wall Street speculators." Chief economist Fatih Birol at the International Energy Agency (IEA) said "Speculators are only responding to what is going on in the markets. We don't see enough oil in the markets. The major driver is supply and demand." Oh really? So then why did the price of oil drop 10% on May 5?!? It trades from $112 down to $98 in a couple of days!? Supply and demand changed that quickly? Maybe the speculators just left the markets completely? Really? This is simply crazy and ridiculous thinking. OPEC is made up of twelve countries that state very clearly that they control 80% of the world's proven oil reserves.

This is what I mean, the markets are controlled and/or manipulated. You do not have to be a genius to figure this out. Just don't be naïve in thinking that we have free markets, because we don't. You will understand this very clearly by the time you are finished reading this book.

Let's take a look at the gold and silver markets since they are getting all the financial headlines lately. As stated earlier, everyday representatives from four major London banking firms (Mocatta & Goldsmid, Samuel Montagu & Co., Sharps Pixley, and Johnson Matheson meet in the offices of NM Rothschild Co. in London to fix the price of gold twice every day. Again, how many analysts, and all these so called gold experts share that with you? How many of your friends actually know this? Heck, I have never read this in any financial news magazine or book. I never was taught this in any financial class in college or graduate school.

On the other hand, silver is much different. Silver can be heavily influenced by Russia, since the Russians account for 70% of the world's production. What attributed to the drop in silver in early May 2011 from near $50 an ounce to $34 an ounce in

4 days was government intervention. The Chicago Mercantile Exchange (CME) hiked the margin requirements for silver contracts purchased on margin rather dramatically. This hurt the smaller traders something terrible. Obviously there were some people that knew this was going to happen, which you will read about later on. They not only profited from selling the metal at high prices, but also in another way.

And so it wasn't supply and demand issues that caused the price of silver to fall like it did, like perhaps many would want you to believe. And nor was it due to speculators.

If you go back to the first two days of May, the price of silver fell $6 in basically ten minutes when virtually all of the world's major markets were closed because of either the time or national holidays. Some traders said this was not a correction but a drive by shooting, and that this was a criminal act which needs to be investigated. Let's just say that here is another example of a market that was manipulated and controlled.

Many of you reading this are familiar with the story about the infamous Hunt Brothers and the silver market. In 1973, the Hunt family was one of the wealthiest families in America and apparently decided to buy silver as a hedge against inflation. Gold was not something that could be held by private citizens at that time. So the Hunt brothers, Nelson and William, along with some wealthy Arabs bought more than 200 million ounces of silver, which was roughly half the world's deliverable supply. Silver was $1.95 an ounce in 1973. By early 1979, the price had reached $5, and by 1980, the price hit $54, a new all time high.

Next thing you know, trading rules changed on the New York Metals Market (COMEX), and the Federal Reserve intervened to put an end to the silver bubble. Prices dropped, culminating in a 50% one day decline on March 27, 1980 as the price dropped from $21.62 to $10.80.

This collapse of the silver market or silver bubble meant huge losses for speculators and countless investors. The Hunt brothers which were one of the wealthiest families in the world, actually had to declare bankruptcy.

Between April 25 and May 5, 2011, margin requirements were increased as much as 12% on silver, resulting in the price dropping from near $50 to $32 an oz.

"In my heart of hearts I believe it was a manipulation" stated Eric Sprott of Sprott Asset Management. "There was no market, it was a setup. They've just pushed it down. It's ridiculous."

Regarding who is directly responsible for the manipulation, Sprott suggests that he believes it is being done by HSBC Bank and JP Morgan. These are the same two major players in the silver market that are being sued in two separate lawsuits by trader Peter Laskaris in federal court.

Let's look at the price of gold which hit an all time high in August of 2011, before margin requirements on trading gold futures were raised dramatically by the CME again. I wonder why. I mean we are all told that we have free markets right? Well then let the free markets set the price. Who told the CME to do this? And why did they do this after gold traded to $1,900 an ounce. Amazing isn't it?

In addition, the Commodity Futures Trading Commission (CFTC) holds that its primary mission is to protect the public from fraud, abuse and manipulation. You have to wonder how much of a drop in the price of silver or gold would it take before the CFTC would comment, investigate, or take some form of action.

The London Metal Exchange (LME) are scrutinizing Goldman

Sachs Group Inc, JP Morgan and other owners of large metals warehouses after being accused by companies like Coca Cola for restricting the amount of metal they release to customers, thereby inflating prices.

Aluminum prices have jumped 13% since the start of 2010 even though economic growth has been declining or flat at best.

It turns out, Goldman, through its Metro International Trade Services unit owns the biggest warehouse in the LME system. They consist of 19 buildings in Detroit that house about a quarter of the aluminum stored in LME facilities.

"The situation has been organized artificially to drive premiums up, said Dave Smith, Atlanta based Coca Cola's strategic procurement manager. "It takes two weeks to put aluminum in, and six months to get it out."

You have to have some sort of understanding that all markets are heavily influenced and/or controlled, because it will help you keep some sort of sanity during chaotic times. Markets can be manipulated by various people or institutions in the extreme short term. People dictate market direction by setting prices or through other econometric measures.

What you are about to read is perhaps the most important chapter in this book and one of the most powerful you may ever read in the area of finance. It has to do with understanding the most powerful entities in the world, particularly when it comes to the area of finance. You have to understand how these entities operate so that you will know how they affect you along with the financial markets. If you know what these powerful entities are doing, then you know whether it's safe to invest or not. This is something that should be taught in every finance class. It isn't in any curriculum because most educators are unaware themselves—

and these entities really do not have any incentive or reason to tell us. It's that simple.

But you need to know what the really **smart money** is doing—and you can only do that by first understanding what these entities are doing.

What are we referring to with the word "entities"? These entities are the central banks. When we talk about the central banks, we are referring to those large banks located in virtually every developed country that dictate monetary policy and heavily influence economies and financial markets. Banks such as the Bank of Japan, the European Central Bank, the Bank of England, the Central Bank of the Russian Federation, the People's Bank of China, and the Federal Reserve (Fed), to name a few. Panama is the only civilized country that we found without a formal central bank.

A central bank is the dominant financial power of the country where it resides. It is privately-owned, yet gives the appearance of a governmental entity. It has the right to issue and print money. It has the ability to provide financing for wars. It operates as a money monopoly with total power over the money and credit of the people.

You may have heard a number of conspiracies regarding the US central bank or the Federal Reserve. There are many books written about the Fed, stirring controversy with many bizarre beliefs. There are even a couple of politicians that have become very vocal and outspoken regarding the Fed and its policies. I have found gross inaccuracies, including quotes taken out of context, along with an assortment of misinformation.

One conspiracy theory about John F. Kennedy alleges that he was assassinated by the Fed because of his desire to abolish the central bank. Actually it had to do with Executive Order 11110, which delegated to the treasury secretary the president's authority to issue silver certificates—paper dollars that were redeemable in silver coins or bullion. The idea was that Kennedy was going to replace Federal Reserve notes with silver certificates, in essence transferring power from the Fed to the Treasury.

In actuality, the order did not expand the issuance of silver certificates, which were in the process of being phased out, especially since rising silver prices could increase redemptions, causing a shortage of the Treasury's silver supply. Kennedy also signed a bill giving the Fed authority to issue small denomination notes to replace the silver certificates. This doesn't sound like Kennedy was exactly trying to abolish the Fed, does it?

One of the other more popular theories is that the New York Federal Reserve really operates the Fed and is principally owned by foreigners. The law states that a small portion of Federal Reserve stock may be available for sale to the public. No person or organization may own more than $25,000 of such public stock and no voting rights (12 USCA 283). Under the Federal Reserve Act, public stock was only to be sold if the sale of stock to member banks that did not raise the minimum of $4 million of capital for each Federal Reserve Bank when they organized in 1913 (12 USCA 281).

Of course each bank was able to raise the necessary amount through member stock sales—and no public stock was ever sold to the non-bank public. No Federal Reserve stock was ever sold to foreigners. It was only sold to banks that are members of the Federal Reserve System. And those banks are public, which means that the SEC requires that all shareholders that control 10 percent or more of the outstanding shares be disclosed, which are then made public. Forget the notion that England or foreigners own the Federal Reserve. Oh really, hold on a second, not so fast, Jack.

The Fed began with approximately thirty-three people or banks that purchased shares in the Fed at $100 a share back in 1914. Their total assets were listed as $143 million. I presume that money was raised from the sale of stock. I say "presume" because it is still a mystery whether or not that money was actually paid by the shareholders or simply was paper issued against paper, bookkeeping entries comprising the only values that changed hands.

Now, these same people own or control the banks that purchased the approximately 10 million shares outstanding in the New York Federal Reserve Bank. This is important because the New York Federal Reserve Bank sets the policy and terms for the rest of the member banks across the country. Therefore, the stockholders of the New York Fed are the real directors of the system and have controlled our political and economic destinies since 1914.

However, because of all the mergers and acquisitions over the past twenty-five years, it doesn't mean much unless we mention the original names that purchased stock in 1914. These names include Chase Manhattan, Citibank, Manufacturers Hanover, European American Bank and Trust, Bankers Trust, J. Henry Schroder Bank & Trust, National Bank of North America, Morgan Guaranty, and Chemical Bank. These names actually control 66 percent of the outstanding shares. If you look at the major stockholders of these banks, it reveals a number of closely related families that hold the controlling stock in the Federal Reserve Bank of New York.

Another interesting note is that three of these banks are subsidiaries of foreign banks. J. Henry Schroder Bank and Trust is a subsidiary of Schroders Ltd. of London. The National Bank of America (now Bank of America) is a subsidiary of the National

Westminster Bank of London. The European America Bank is a subsidiary of the European American Bank, Bahamas, Ltd.

Further investigation shows that the Chairman of J. Henry Schroder of London just happened to be the head of the Bank of England. The ties to the Bank of England are interesting.

Investors need to know fact from fiction; this is the foundation for understanding how the financial system operates.

Now you see who really owns these entities or central banks. These banks are not wholly owned by the governments that they purportedly represent. When you research the families that own the majority of the shares in these banks, some common names appear, including Rothschild, Rockefeller, JP Morgan, Lazard Freres, Schroder, Warburg, and Loeb. Rockefellers own the majority of shares in Chase Manhattan Bank. That's right; this is not by coincidence or chance. This is all about power and control.

In this country, we are going to closely examine the Federal Reserve. The Federal Reserve is not really a government entity as most people think and as we are led to believe. It operates like a private corporation. There are no reserves—and it operates in secret.

The Federal Reserve Banks are not federal instrumentalities...
—Lewis vs. United States

The Federal Reserve banks, while not part of the government...
—United States budget for 1991 and 1992, part 7, page 10

The Federal Reserve consists of twelve regional banks and a board of governors. The board of governors consists of 7 members. It is organized with a government agency at the top (the board of governors) and branches beneath them that resemble private corporations.

The board of governors are appointed by the president and confirmed by Congress. They are appointed to fourteen-year terms. The board operates per its charter and laws set by Congress. There is no private ownership at this level. In fact, board members are forbidden by law to have any economic ownership in a private bank.

The twelve branches, however, are organized like private corporations. Member banks are required to buy shares in their branch. The shares come with a 6 percent dividend.[6] These shares cannot be sold, traded, or pledged as security for a loan. The profit made from the Federal Reserve branches goes to the Treasury at the end of the year, which the Fed has been doing since 1947. Is this private ownership? The Feds say no, but the courts say that the branch operation is treated as a private corporation.

> *The regional Federal Reserve Banks are not government agencies… but are independent, privately owned and locally controlled corporations.*
> —Lewis vs. United States, 680 F.2d 1239, 9th Circuit, 1982

The amount of shares owned by private banks in the Federal Reserve is not well publicized—to say the least. The law states that member banks must purchase shares equal to 6 percent of their capital and surplus. If you know the total banking assets (around $5 trillion) and you look at the assets of the biggest banks, you can get an idea of their Fed shares.
For example:

---

6   www.federalreserve.gov

Bank of America: $1.3 billion in total assets or about 20 percent

JP Morgan: $1.1 billion in total assets or about 20 percent

The rest of the shares are split among the other 2,500 member banks. [7]

These twelve corporations together cover the whole country and monopolize and use for private gain every dollar of the public currency...
—Mr. Alfred Owen Crozier, before the Senate Banking and Currency Committee, 1913

Some people think the Federal Reserve Banks are the United States government's institutions. They are not government institutions. They are private credit monopolies which prey upon the people of the United States for the benefit of themselves and their foreign swindlers.
—Congressional Record 12595-12603 Louis T. McFadden, Chairman of the Committee on Banking and Currency, June 10, 1932

Now you know that most of the important public policy decisions in the United States are not being made in any public forum or even by elected officials. They are being made in secret by unelected officials from the board of governors of the Federal Reserve—the Federal Advisory Council.

Our Fed seems to promote financial instability in the United States. An official memo from the board on March 13, 1939 stated that: "The board of governors of the Federal Reserve System

---

7 www.federalreserve.gov

opposes any bill which proposes a stable price level." Isn't this just wonderful? At least you know now.

The Federal Reserve Bank of New York is the bank that really dictates policy and terms to the rest of the member banks.

During the summer of 2010 when news hit that Greece was having debt issues, the central bankers met in secret at a secret location in Australia. Why don't we know where they met or what was discussed that weekend? And who specifically are these people? What they decide and discuss influences and affects all of us. Who is their boss? Who do they report to and who are they accountable to? I certainly do not have these answers.

Let's look at the numbers. On August 31, 2009, the Federal Reserve announced that they made $14 billion in profits on loans made in the prior two years, reported the *Financial Times*. The central bank also made about $19 billion from interest and fees charged to institutions that tapped liquidity facilities during the financial crisis, the report stated. If the Fed had invested the same amount loaned out in three-month Treasury bills since August 2007, it would have earned only $5 billion in interest, the *Financial Times* reported. Think for a second. Would you like to make $5 billion or $33 billion? That huge difference is significant enough for you to understand what occurred in 2008–2009 in the United States.

We have to examine this situation because it's important that you understand how the central bank works. First, who keeps the money that was made on the loans? It is returned to the Treasury, which in turn helps to lower our deficit. Do you mean to tell me that they made $33 billion in less than two years?

Now just think for a minute —how do you get institutions to want to borrow money and lots of it? Perhaps a widespread panic might do the trick. How many institutions were forced to take

TARP funds? And after they did, how many wanted to give them back and the government didn't want to take them?

During the 2008 political election, we were constantly told about how big our budget deficit was. Doesn't that mean the government needs money? And they don't want to take back monies from the banks? Now why is that? For control reasons, perhaps? Maybe because the Fed wanted to make money by loaning money?

In 2009, the Fed reported making $50 billion. In 2010, the Fed earned $81 billion, of which $78.4 billion was remitted to the Treasury. A total of $1.6 billion was paid as dividends to member banks—and $600 million was retained to "equate surplus with paid in capital."[8] To put things in perspective, this represents a 90% increase over the FED's 2007 pre-financial crisis profit of $38.7 billion.

To top it all off, the FED uses its own outdated accounting protocols, rather than GAAP, or generally accepted accounting practices, used by every other governmental agency and business. In addition, no quarterly earnings reports are ever issued. How is that for transparency? Every bank in the US reports , but not the FED? This means the Fed's business escapes public and congressional scrutiny. Now you know a little about the world's most profitable company.

The United States government paid $413 billion in interest in 2010 on our national debt. It was transferred from taxpayers to the United States government and then transferred from the United States government to big financial institutions, foreign countries, and bankers. This is what is going on all over the world. Since

---

8   www.federalreserve.org

sovereign governments are drowning in debt, they drain their taxpayers dry to meet their obligations.

A former governor of the Federal Reserve Board, Marriner Eccles, stated before the House and Banking and Currency Committee years ago that, "Debt is the basis for the creation of money."

> *It is well enough that people of the nation do not understand banking and monetary system, for if they did, I believe there would be a revolution before tomorrow morning. The one aim of these financiers is world control by the creation of inextinguishable debt.*
> *—Henry Ford*

> *Most Americans have no real understanding of the operation of the international money lenders. The accounts of the Federal Reserve have never been audited. It operates outside the control of Congress and manipulates the credit of the United States.*
> *—Senator Barry Goldwater, Arizona*

> *The Federal Reserve banks are one of the most corrupt institutions the world has ever seen. There is not a man within the sound of my voice who does not know that this nation is run by the international bankers.*
> *—Congressman Louis McFadden, Pennsylvania*

What would you think if the FED bailed out a foreign bank? Totally not cool, right? Well, that's what the New York Federal Reserve Bank did from December 2008 – December 2009. According to a report from the Government Accounting Office, loans were made to Swiss central bankers to buy assets from a Swiss bank. With all the so- called US banks that were in trouble, we are lending money overseas? This could easily have escalated into a huge scandal if people knew that our central bankers were bailing out a foreign bank.

Just understand that the Federal Reserve has similar agreements with other countries as well. The point is that quite often these central bankers are working together, and our own central bank operates independently and in its own best interests, not our country's or yours or mine.

There you have it. The Federal Reserve is not really a federal or a government entity. It is not owned by our government, but by people that own and control the large banks that directly own shares in the New York Federal Reserve Bank. These shares are controlled by a number of people, many of which live both in the US and maintain distinct ties to England.

The New York Federal Reserve Bank sets interest rates and is in charge of all open-market operations for the entire Federal Reserve System. There are no reserves. Our government doesn't own a single share of stock in the Fed and has no real system. A syndicate of families dictates and controls our economy and financial markets.

The Federal Reserve System in the United States is really no different from other central banks, such as the Bank of England or the Bank of France.

Before you think you know everything about the Federal Reserve in the US…wait! The very first audit of the Federal Reserve came public with all kinds of interesting information on September 27, 2011. It was the very first audit conducted by the Government Accountability Office or GAO. Now before you get too excited, it wasn't a complete audit. I too had to sit back down when I read that it wasn't a complete audit like I had hoped. Even so, what they found was simply amazing.

"As a result of this audit, we now know that the Federal Reserve provided more than $16 trillion in total financial assistance to some of the largest financial institutions and corporations in the United States and throughout the world," stated Senator Bernie Sanders. Senator Sanders was responsible for an amendment to the Dodd-Frank reform bill which called for the audit.

The findings found that the Federal Reserve provided trillions of dollars from South Korea to Scotland. "No agency of the United States government should be allowed to bailout a foreign bank or corporation without the direct approval of Congress and the president," Sanders stated.

The conflicts of interest here are utterly amazing, which makes me think that the protests that appeared around the world against the Wall St excesses should really have been aimed more towards the banks and the Federal Reserve. If the people only knew.

Take for example the CEO of JP Morgan Chase, Jaime Dimon. He served on the New York Fed's board of directors at the same time that his bank received more than $390 billion in financial assistance from the Fed. And get this, JP Morgan Chase served as one of the clearing banks for the Fed's emergency lending programs.

The report also showed that on September 19, 2008, William Dudley, who is now the New York Fed president, was granted a waiver to let him keep investments in AIG and GE at the same time they both were given bailout funds. The audit showed that the Fed did not make Dudley sell his holdings because of the fact that it might have created the appearance of a conflict of interest. Are you kidding me? What is this?

The audit also revealed that the Fed outsourced most of its

emergency lending programs to private contractors, many of which also received very low interest and secret loans.

Something else you need to understand is that much of the information that we have shared with you was not easy to find. The Federal Reserve is indeed a mystery to most Americans as is most central banks to their own respective citizenry. So, it can be difficult to find out what the Fed is doing, but it is important that you have some idea and pay attention to what they are doing. Much of the Fed's activities as well as most central banks is secret. Don't believe me?

There is an organization that seeks to expose, oppose, and litigate against anyone that attempts to control the supply and price of gold. It is the Gold Anti-Trust Action Committee or (GATA). GATA wanted access to the Fed's gold-related records. This in turn led the Fed to admit that they actually do have gold swap arrangements with foreign banks and wanted to keep them secret. GATA sued the Fed in US District Court in the District of Columbia in December 2009, attempting to obtain these records. However in February 2011, the court ruled that most of the Fed's gold records could remain secret. Imagine that. However, one did have to be revealed: the April 2007 minutes from the Group of Ten or G-10[9] member treasury and central bank official secret meeting to co-ordinate their policies towards the gold market. The court did order the Fed to pay court costs to GATA, but that was it.

The G-10 by the way refers to the group of countries that have agreed to participate in the General Agreements to Borrow (GAB). The GAB was set up in 1962, when ten countries: Belgium, France, Canada, Italy, Japan, Sweden, Switzerland, United

---

9   IMF (www.imf.org/external/np/exr/facts/groups.htm)

Kingdom, United States, and the Netherlands agreed to make monies available to the International Monetary Fund (IMF).

Now you should have a pretty good understanding who controls the broader markets through their ability to set fiscal and monetary policies. This is important to understand because it gives you insight and perspective on the financial markets as a whole.

However, when it comes to specific markets, you also understand that there are specific groups, companies, and or individuals that largely influence specific markets. There are trading houses that form a very exclusive group. They are so big that they are worth well over a trillion dollars according to many reports. They are responsible for trading more than half the world's freely traded commodities. They influence markets by amassing huge positions in raw goods, hoard commodities in warehouses, and oil in super-tankers. They also own mines, ships, pipelines, warehouses, silos, and ports where they store commodities.

Commodities markets are mostly free of insider trading restrictions. These trading houses operate with inside knowledge, and connections that enable them to operate as power brokers, especially in emerging markets of Africa, Asia, and Latin America.

"The payout percentage of profits at the commodities houses can be double what Wall Street banks pay," says George Stein of New York headhunting firm Commodity Talent.

Glencore which recently went public, headquartered in Switzerland pays some traders yearly bonuses in the tens of millions.

Two of the biggest trading houses are Vitrol and Trafigura. They are so big that the two of them sold a combined 8.1 million barrels of oil in one day in 2010. By comparison that is equal to the combined exports of Saudi Arabia and Venezuela.

Vitol's sales in 2010 were $195 billion!!!!! Twice those of Apple! It also owns 200 tankers at sea and storage tanks all over the world.

US regulators are cracking down on big banks and hedge funds that speculate in commodities, but trading firms remain largely unregulated. Many are unlisted and are often based in such tax havens as Switzerland. These are giant companies that broker the world's basic goods. They operate very secretly and quietly.

In fact Vitrol just supplied Libyan rebels with $1 billion in fuel according to Reuters. Supplies which were desperately needed to advance on Tripoli. In return, Libyan oil firm Agoco allocated Vitol half of its crude production to repay the debt. Vitol along with Trafigura kept refined product supplies flowing to the besieged government of Bashar al-Assad in Syria as government troops attacked its citizens. Trading houses could do this because international sanctions on Syria do not ban the sale of fuel into the country.

"There has always been some concern about the trading firms influence," stated Craig Pirrong, finance professor and commodities specialist at the University of Houston. Pirrong also states that some firms "have been associated with allegations of market manipulation."

Remember when oil prices hit almost $150 a barrel in 2007? Prices are supposed to rise according to Economics 101 when there is increased demand. Supply and demand are supposed to determine prices for things, right? Well, our demand for oil didn't skyrocket in 2007, so why did prices rise so dramatically? Well, in May 2011, the US Commodity Futures Trading Commission sued the giant trading firms (Arcadia and Parnon) for allegedly manipulating US oil prices, amassing millions of barrels of oil that they had no intention of using.

Executives of Illinois based Archer Daniels Midland were jailed for an early international price-fixing conspiracy for an animal feed additive lysine.

US oil refiner Tosco sued Arcadia and Glencore for market manipulation. The case was settled out of court.

There are a total of sixteen trading firms that heavily influence and control commodity prices around the world. However, there are only six trading firms which own huge warehouses that store metals. You see stock in warehouses can be tied up for years as loan collateral, allowing the same traders who dominate the metals market to control a huge chunk of world supply. These firm's names are worth noting due to the strong commodities market and interest by many investors with metals. If you want to know where metals prices are going, find out what these six trading firms are doing. Steinweg, Glencore, Trafigura, Noble, Goldman Sachs, and JP Morgan are the firms.

These trading firms don't just make money when commodity prices rise. They make considerable amounts from arbitrage. What they do is trade on the divergence in prices at different locations, between different future delivery dates, and the commodity's quality at different locations.

This is what many of the trading firms did in 2009 when they parked 100 million barrels of oil in super tankers. Then a trading scenario known as contango evolved. A process whereby buyers pay more for future delivery than to receive their goods right away. These trading firms would sell futures and lock in profits of $10 or more per barrel of oil!

Not only do you now know that the commodities markets

are heavily influenced and/or controlled, but you know who the names of some of the firms responsible and the methods that they use. It is important that you know this if you are really interested in investing in commodities, because you have to know what the big money, in essence the quiet money, what we call **Smart Money** is doing. It is equally important in knowing who the major players are that heavily influence and/or control markets that you may want to invest in. It is amazing to me just how many licensed financial professionals do not know this. Wall St. certainly does not exactly advertise, promote, or educate its financial professionals as to why and how things happen.

Historical Perspective

Historical perspective is important because it will help you form a frame of reference that you will see is still relevant in understanding what takes place in our financial markets.

We know people have experienced countless difficult and economic hardships; they are nothing new. We all know about the Great Depression and the stock market crash of 1929. But did you know that there were other depressions and financial panics all the way back to 1800? We will look at the financial panic and the depressions of 1893 and 1907. What is interesting is that these panics and depressions all have a couple of things in common.

First, the financial panic and depression in 1893 in the United States was attributed to railroad overbuilding and shaky railroad financing that set off a series of bank failures. The railroad bubble burst, causing a run on the gold supply and a policy of using both gold and silver metals as a peg for the value of the dollar.

The decline of gold reserves stored in the Treasury fell to a dangerously low level, forcing President Cleveland to borrow $65 million in gold from banker JP Morgan in order to support the gold standard.

The panic in 1907, also known as the Banker's Panic, occurred when the New York Stock Exchange (NYSE) fell close to 50 percent from its previous year's peak. Panic ensued, and there was a run on numerous banks and trust companies. In fact, the NYSE's governing board voted to close the exchange for up to five months. JP Morgan Sr. specifically forbade an early closure of the exchange, but to no avail.

The panic really started when the attempt failed to corner the market on the United Copper Company. As soon as this bid failed, banks that had lent huge amounts of money to the cornering scheme suffered runs that later spread to other affiliated banks and trusts.

The panic would have been a lot worse had it not been for JP Morgan. Morgan convinced other bankers such as John Rockefeller to inject large sums of money into the banking system.

Also worth noting is that a large company, Tennessee Coal, Iron, and Railroad Company (TC&I), had their stock heavily shorted, which severely dropped its share price. A total collapse of its stock price was averted by an emergency takeover from Morgan's United States Steel Corporation. This is an example of manipulation that still goes on today—as you will soon read. Remember this because you will not believe the similarities with what happened with TC&I and what occurred in 2008 to Washington Mutual and Bear Stearns.

What caused the stock market crash of 1929 and the Great Depression? There are probably many different theories and thoughts regarding just what led up to this. We know that Europe wanted our gold in order to force its nations back to the gold standard. We moved $500 million of gold to Europe, which in turn deflated the stock market, ended business prosperity, and sunk us into the Great Depression. We can only surmise that the bankers wanted the Great Depression because it put the business and finance of the United States in their hands. It is a very terrible thought, but it is logical nonetheless.

WHERE IT REALLY ALL STARTED

Even after 1907, there were still anxieties about America's ability to avoid another financial crisis. In 1913, a few men representing the wealthiest families from around the world left a train station in Hoboken, New Jersey, in Senator Nelson Aldrich's private rail car to Jekyll Island, Georgia, supposedly to duck hunt. Jekyll Island offered complete privacy for these men—not a journalist for miles. Reportedly, no last names were used at any time during the nearly two-week stay at the Jekyll Island Club Hotel. It was said that nearly one-sixth of the entire world's wealth was represented at the meetings. One of the families was represented by John Paul Morgan, the financier whose name you certainly now recognize. Morgan was credited with paving the way for what is now known as the Federal Reserve.

The stated purpose of the Federal Reserve, according to its website, is to "conduct the nation's monetary policy by influencing money and credit conditions in the economy in pursuit of full employment and stable prices."[10]

From 1776–1912, the value of the dollar increased by 11

---

10   www.federalreserve.gov

percent. That means that a loaf of bread for Thomas Jefferson cost the same as a loaf of bread for Abraham Lincoln fifty years later and again the same for John Pierpont Morgan fifty years after that. After the Federal Reserve was created, the value of the dollar decreased 95 percent from 1913–2008. If you had $1,000,000 in 1913, it would be worth just $50,000 today.[11]

The value of the dollar was relatively stable for 150 years before the creation of the Federal Reserve. Since then, we have seen a 95 percent devaluation of the dollar in less than a hundred years since its creation. Below is a graph from 1900–2010 depicting the history of the United States dollar.

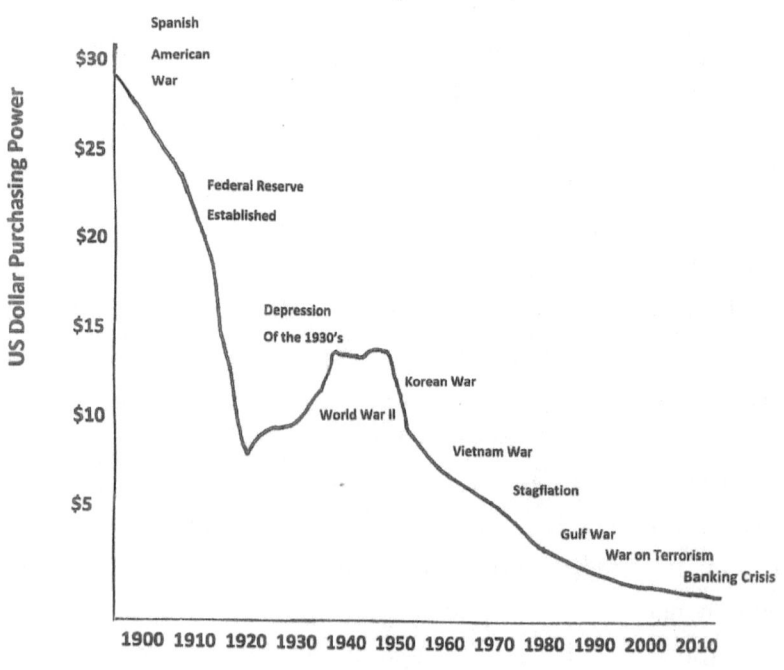

US $ Decline in Spending Power
The Rise and Fall of the US $ Dollar

---

11   Goldseek.com, LewRockwell.com

We are led to believe that inflation is always present or something that just happens in our economy, but that is not true. Inflation, which is the lost spending power of your dollar, can largely be attributed to the Federal Reserve's mismanagement of the money supply.

Every Congressman, every Senator knows precisely what causes inflation ... but can't (won't) support the drastic reforms to stop it (Repeal of the Federal Reserve Act) because it could cost him his job.
—Robert A. Heinlein, Expanded Universe

We all should be extremely upset over the kind of influence that they have over our dollar, in essence your net worth.

Whoever controls the volume of money in any country is absolute master of all industry and commerce.
—James Garfield, former president of the United States

President Obama is mandating that the Federal Reserve have more oversight, authority, and control over American financial markets—and that is exactly what is taking place. You should probably expect that to continue as well.

It was the very first US President, George Washington that stated, **"Paper money has had the effect in your state that it will ever have, to ruin commerce, oppress the honest, and open the door to every species of fraud and injustice."**

"We may become a great commercial and flourishing nation. But if in the pursuit of the means we should unfortunately stumble again on unfounded paper money or any similar species of fraud, we shall assuredly give a fatal stab to our national credit in its infancy." Sounds like a quote from someone last week or last month, not from over 200 years ago.

Much destruction and devastation occurred in our financial market and country in 2008. What took years to build vanished in less than a year. Trillions of dollars were gone—quite possibly forever.

A look back in history will shed some perspective. One of the biggest financial scams in the world (prior to 2008) occurred more than 250 years ago, but few people know anything about it. What you are about to read is not taught in business schools or financial textbooks—and you certainly won't hear anything about it in today's financial press.

It all happened in England in 1815. Nathan Rothschild deceived British investors into believing that the Duke of Wellington had lost to Napoleon at the Battle of Waterloo. In a few short hours, British government bonds literally crashed, and Rothschild, who had advanced insider information, bought up the entire market in government bonds for pennies on the pound. Over the course of the nineteenth century, Rothschild became the biggest bank in the world.

I care not what puppet is placed on the throne of England to rule the Empire… The man that controls Britain's money supply controls the British Empire. And I control the money supply, stated Nathan Rothschild in 1815

Let me issue and control a nation's money and I care not who writes the laws.
—Nathan Rothschild, 1838

In 1907, another panic was triggered by rumors that two major banks were going under. John Pierpont Morgan deceived the public into believing that the banks would go under and a run on the banks quickly ensued. Morgan then nobly stepped in to avert the panic by importing $100 million in gold from Europe.

Soon thereafter, the public became convinced that the country needed a central banking system to prevent future panics. Congress had been opposed to any legislation that would allow the nation's money to be issued by a private central bank controlled by Wall Street. However, after the meeting in Jekyll Island, the Federal Reserve was created and the Federal Reserve Act—also known as the Aldrich Plan—was passed in 1913. Senator Nelson Aldrich, (maternal grandfather to the Rockefellers) pushed the act through Congress just before Christmas when many members were already on vacation.

John Pierpont Morgan created the conditions for the Federal Reserve Act's passage, but it was actually a German banker, Paul Warburg, who pulled it off. The 1931 book *Roosevelt, Wilson and the Federal Reserve Law* says, "Paul Warburg is the man who got the Federal Reserve Act together after the Aldrich Plan aroused such nationwide resentment and opposition." Warburg didn't want the term central bank used, so he proposed the Federal Reserve System. Warburg's plan consisted of a board of governors that would be appointed by the president of the United States, but the real work would be controlled by the Federal Advisory Council, meeting with the governors. The council would be chosen by the directors of the twelve Federal Reserve Banks, and would remain unknown to the public.

The Federal Reserve officially began operations on November 16, 1914.

> *This (Federal Reserve Act) establishes the most gigantic trust on earth. When the president signs this bill, the invisible government of the monetary power will be legalized ... the worst legislative crime of the ages is perpetrated by this banking and currency bill.*
> —*Charles Lindbergh Sr., 1913*

This holds the key to what recently occurred in the United States.

Robert Owens, co-author of the Federal Reserve Act, testified before Congress that the banking industry had conspired to create a series of financial panics in order to motivate the public to demand "reforms" that served the interest of the bankers.[12] Nearly one hundred years later, JP Morgan may have changed the course of history again. This bank acquired the nation's largest residential mortgage lender (Washington Mutual) and the nation's most profitable investment banker (Bear Stearns) for pennies on the dollar, using the same tactics as they had before. Tell me that history doesn't repeat itself. It's kind of funny that no other banks were allowed to participate or make a play for Bear Stearns or Washington Mutual. This didn't occur by accident, chance, or coincidence.

Woodrow Wilson signed the creation of the Federal Reserve into law in 1913.

> *I have unwittingly ruined my country. A great industrial nation is controlled by its system of credit. Our system of credit is concentrated in the hands of a few men. We have come to be one of the worst ruled, one of the most completely controlled and dominated governments in the world ... no*

---

12 thehiddenevil.com

> *longer a government of free opinion, no longer a government by conviction and vote of the majority, but a government by opinion and duress of small groups of dominant men.*
> —Woodrow Wilson

> *I believe that banking institutions are more dangerous to our liberties than standing armies. Already they have raised up a monied aristocracy that has set the government at defiance. The issuing power (of money) should be taken away from the banks and restored to the people to whom it properly belongs.*
> —Thomas Jefferson

The founders of the United States clearly opposed central banking. In fact, the Constitution says Congress "shall have the power to coin money, regulate the value thereof, and of foreign coin." You should now understand how the central banks operate and influence financial markets and economies. In 1994, the Federal Reserve's vice chairman, Alan Blinder, stated, "The last duty of a central banker is to tell the public the truth."[13]

Can you believe that? This is incredible. Arm yourself with this information and you will be able to think your way through difficult times—and navigate your way through your investments when the financial panics occur. You should now begin to have a better understanding of how we got here as a country financially speaking. More importantly, how and why things happen economically, which affect each and every one of us. All planned, and carefully executed.

---

13 masternewmedia.org

THE 2008 ECONOMIC CRISIS

Influential Media

Fabricated? Well planned, well thought out, or maybe something just quickly conjured up? However you think things happened, one fact remains. The economy and stock market went down hill and quickly. In fact, things got far worse than most people imagined, including me.

Up until early 2008, all the economic news throughout the free world was very positive, particularly here in the US. Economic indicators like job growth, inflation, and GDP numbers were positive. Consumer confidence was high. The US stock market (the DOW) hit an all time high of over 14,400. Businesses were hiring and prospering, and the US appeared to be doing quite well.

So how could things change so rapidly and so quickly? I mean how could things go from so good in 2007 to so bad in 2008 in less than a year?

Well you don't need to understand why things happened, as much as you need to understand the way they did. The media had a crucial role in reporting the news as it usually does. It is just that this time the magnitude of what took place and the amount of misinformation given to the public was immense. The media was used to help orchestrate a number of changes within our economy and with our markets. All of which had important lasting repercussions for our economy, for the US, and for each US citizen.

> *From now on, depressions will be scientifically created.*
> *—Congressman Charles Lindbergh Sr., 1913*

Remember that nothing happens by accident, chance, or coincidence when it comes to politics and finance. It's not by accident that our economy went south in 2008. Think for a minute about just how orchestrated and orderly this all was. It may not have seemed like it when we were being inundated with all sorts of negativity, gloom, and doom. The media focused on job losses and how bad things were in the United States and overseas. You never read anything that happened in 2008 that was even remotely positive.

Forget politics here for a moment. Before all the economic gloom, all we heard and saw in the news for the prior six years focused on every time someone died in Iraq. Well did you ever wonder why you didn't hear of people dying in other parts of the world, like in parts of Africa where more people can die in a week than die in a year in Iraq? Or maybe why you hear very little or nothing about the major offensives in Afghanistan where our men continue to die, where is the media coverage? In fact, you really do not hear about our war in Afghanistan or the men and women that are dying at all. Do you see the change/changes?

Your neighbor probably doesn't even know that we are fighting a war in Afghanistan—the same goes for the general public in this country. There is a reason for this—it doesn't occur by chance or by mistake. Doesn't it make you wonder why you don't see or hear of any protests over the war? It is strange to go from one extreme to the other extreme so quickly and quietly. Am I the only one that has noticed this?

It is critically important to understand that the American media is controlled just as it is in many countries. You will not find balanced, objective information as you might have come to expect. The news is often used for a specific reason or to seek a specific outcome.

> *Our job is not to give people what they want,*
> *but what we decide they ought to have.*
> *—Richard Salant, former president, CBS News*

Here is another example in case you are still not convinced about the mass media. How many times have you heard about how the United States is hardly manufacturing anything at all and that the United States has become a second-rate power?

In reality, nothing could be further from the truth. The facts paint a completely different picture. The United States is still the world's leading manufacturer. In 2007, goods produced totaled a record $1.6 trillion, almost double the $811 billion produced a decade earlier. In a rare story in February 2009, Stephen Manning of the Associated Press said, "For every $1 of value produced in China's factories [in 2007], America generated $2.50."

In fact, the United States leads the world in many high-value fields, producing more than half of the $175 billion in health care technology products purchased worldwide in 2008. The United States also ranks as the world's largest chemical producer, in addition to selling more than $200 billion worth of aircraft, missiles, and space-related equipment in 2007."[14]

---

14 MSNBC.com

In the midst of a global recession, the United States exported an estimated $3.77 trillion worth of goods in 2010, according to the authoritative CIA World Factbook.

We all know that negative news sells, but it's more than that. You will not find any other country where the news can be as negative as in the United States.

In Dubai, the media is not allowed to convey anything that would have a negative impact on the country's economy or currency. Why do you think that is? Is it any wonder that Dubai has achieved unprecedented growth and prosperity in such a short period of time?

Dubai has the world's largest shopping mall and the world's tallest building. The country continues to work on some incredible and amazing technological feats in construction.

What would happen if our country took the same stance as Dubai? We would probably see some dramatic changes and direction in the United States.

Politicians, special interest groups, and the people behind the scenes typically find it much easier to move their agendas forward during times of extreme negativism and despair. Many dramatic changes took place in our country, particularly during 2008 and 2009, but many of them deliberately fuel the public's anxiety to advance their agendas. Be alert to this because it's important to decipher fact from fiction. It does not matter whether it is the general news media or the financial news media. Be aware, and do not fall prey to what they want the masses to believe, or to respond in a certain way. If you have noticed, there are more programs designed to bring the intelligence level of Americans lower. Whether you like it or not, it is happening. You can see it in the public school systems, the pure lack of education, and dramatic changes in curriculum. American history is simply disappearing from school textbooks. You see it in the adult cartoons on television now. When was the last time you saw a high school student reading a book, instead of gaming or texting, that is in the US of course.

In 2010, we all constantly heard in the financial press or media about the number of bank failures. The latest headline, "Florida bank fails, 40th shuttered in 2011" by Associated Press on May 7, 2011 is such an example. [15]There were actually 140 bank failures in 2009, and 157 in 2010. You might think that this is incredible stuff and just terrible. Well, it isn't good, that is for sure. The point here is that if you were to put things in perspective, this wouldn't be so alarming. In 1988-1989, more than 1000 banks failed!!! That's right.

We all saw or heard of emails that were circulated in 2008-2009 regarding how there would be a run on the banks, similar to 1929-1930 during the Great Depression. These have died out for now, but I had seen countless number of alarming emails from so called analysts, and talk show hosts claiming such.

Have you ever noticed what happens to the failed bank? In most cases, another bank has already been contacted, and the deal consummated by the time the press announces the failure. The FDIC will seize the bank, and another bank will assume deposits and buy the assets. Terms of which are rarely disclosed. Any losses are shared with the new bank and the FDIC. The point is that you don't want to be fooled or deceived by the mass media or by just reading the headlines. You need to read between the lines and do your own homework.

Now, there certainly have been many dramatic changes that have taken place in our country, particularly during some extreme

---

15 Associated Press, May 6, 2011

forms of negativism and despair, like we experienced in 2008 and 2009.

Our country is becoming very similar to much of Western Europe in many ways. Our stock market and foreign markets are now closely correlated. We are becoming more like the rest of the world day by day. This trend appears as if it may continue for some time. What? You think this is crazy and ridiculous? I did too until I did more research. I slowly came to understand what is happening right before our very eyes. The large banks that control all the assets will not lend to small businesses, so you do not see the job creation like you would normally expect to see. This ain't by accident! This is going to very quickly destroy the middle class in the US. In fact, there are some predicting that the US could become a third world country before you know it. This is why we have illegal immigration and will not secure our border with Mexico. Don't believe me? Go look and see what happens to you if you were to illegally enter Mexico or China. This you could say is all part of this New World Order.

> *We shall have world government whether or not you like it ... by conquest or consent.*
> —*James Warburg, Rothschild banking agent and financial adviser to Franklin D. Roosevelt, 1950*

Some even believe we (the Rockefeller family) are part of a secret cabal working against the best interests of the United States, characterizing my family and me as "internationalists" and of conspiring with others around the world to build a more integrated global political and economic structure- one world, if you will. If that's the charge, I stand guilty, and I am proud of it.
—*David Rockefeller*

THE FINANCIAL MARKET MELTDOWN

Naked Shorting

To get a proper perspective on what happened to our country and to our markets, one can just simply focus on what role the **smart money** played. As we stated earlier, nothing in the financial world happens by accident. What took place in 2008 was an absolute travesty for all American citizens and investors alike. We have never seen anything even remotely similar to this market since the 1920s.

In the fall of 2007, the Dow made a new all time high. Everything seemed ok. The leading economic indicators were all positive like job growth, productivity numbers, GDP (gross domestic product). We all know that the stock market is supposed to be a direct reflection of the economy. Both the market and the economy were all doing well just when the financial landscape was about to change in ways never thought imaginable.

We all know that Wall St. investment banks packaged and marketed a number of derivatives which were then sold to banks around the world. These derivatives you know as CDO's (collateralized debt obligations), and CMO's (collateralized mortgage obligations) just to name a few. These derivatives as we all know turned out to be huge losses for many banks. However, according to the Permanent Subcommittee on Investigations report on the financial crisis, "Goldman Sachs created new securities, backed them with its good name, and then strung together misleading statements to its customers about what it was actually doing. By shorting the way it did, the bank perverted the market instead of correcting it."

According to a New York Times article from June 15, 2011, "Goldman's techniques harmed the capital markets. Goldman brought something into the world that didn't exist before. Instead of selling something-thereby decreasing the price or supply of it- and giving the market a signal that it was less desirable, Goldman did the opposite. The firm created more mortgage investments and gave the world the signal that there was more demand, for CDO's and for the mortgages that backed them."

The article states, "By shorting CDO's, Goldman also distorted the pricing of the underlying assets. The bank could have taken the securities it owned and sold them en masse in a fairly negotiated sale, though it likely would have gotten less for them than it was able to make by shorting the CDO's it created."

"Because of Goldman's actions, the financial system took greater losses than there otherwise would have been. Goldman's form of shorting prolonged the boom and made the crisis that followed much worse, "the Times stated.

However there is more to what caused the economic crisis in the US than simply the financial derivative losses. Secretly and very quietly the SEC allowed a handful of hedge funds that control over $2 trillion in assets the ability to do something that no one else was allowed or permitted to do. What are we talking about?

It has to do with selling short naked—something that should not have been allowed by anyone. The consequences were devastating to companies, our country, our markets, and individual investors.

Regular short selling is legal and occurs when you sell a stock that has been borrowed by a third party with the intent of buying the identical stock back at a later date to return to the lender. Or stated simpler, it is selling a stock that you don't own—or any sale that is completed by the delivery of a security borrowed by the seller.

Naked short selling is different in that you just sell, sell, and sell as many shares as you want. And you don't have to borrow those shares—all you have to do is sell. This practice hasn't occurred in the United States since the 1920s when JP Morgan was practicing naked short selling with many banks, trying to force them out of business. It took an act of Congress to stop it. If people had been aware of this, perhaps similar measures would have been taken. Again, this is an example of **smart money**. Two trillion dollars making huge sums of money in hedge funds while the average investor is losing, and our country losing big. What happened in 2008 was contrived and well orchestrated by many parties.

You need to know how this really works. In recent years, a number of companies have been accused of using naked shorts in aggressive efforts to drive down share prices—sometimes with no intention of even delivering the shares. In theory, this practice allows an unlimited number of shares to be sold short. A *Los Angeles Times* article in July 2008 stated that naked short selling "enables speculators to drive down a company's stock price by offering an overwhelming number of shares for sale."

Let's apply this to the recent share price collapse with a couple of stocks. Citigroup and AIG, which both collapsed, each traded in excess of a billion shares in a single day to the downside. No stock—we repeat—no stock ever traded this many shares in a single day in the United States! Yet there was no mention of it anywhere in the press!

Back in 2008-2009, the US stock market would trade a billion to a billion and a half shares in an average trading day. I watched AIG and Citigroup each trade over a billion shares in a single day! And when they did, each was down a tremendous percentage amount. You got it. Naked short selling. I also observed this type of short selling in Bank of America, decimating the market cap and taking the stock down to nearly $2 a share from $14 a share in March 2009. Never had I ever witnessed such a deliberate and massive price manipulation in stocks like I saw with this naked shorting. Lehman Brothers and Bear Stearns were two others that were obvious targets and victims.

The SEC says that naked shorting is sometimes falsely asserted as a reason for a share price decline when, in fact, "the price decrease is a result of the company's poor financial situation rather than the reasons provided by the insiders or promoters."[16]

Robert J. Shapiro (former undersecretary of commerce for economic affairs and a consultant to a law firm suing over naked shorting) has claimed that naked shorting has cost investors $100 billion and driven 1,000 companies into the ground.[17]

We want you to understand just how dangerous and detrimental to investing it is when naked short selling is allowed to occur. You have to be aware of it—or you will lose money by blindly investing.

In July 2005, the SEC announced emergency actions to limit

---

16 wikipedia.org
17 *Time*, November 9, 2005

the naked short selling of government-sponsored enterprises (GSE's) such as Fannie Mae and Freddie Mac in an effort to decrease the volatility.

But even with respect to these stocks, the SEC soon announced that there would be an exception with regard to market-makers. This rule expired August 12, 2005.

However on September 17, 2008, the SEC issued new, more extensive rules against naked shorting, making "it crystal clear that the SEC has zero tolerance for abusive naked short selling."[18] One of the new rules says that market-makers are no longer given an exception. As a result, options market-makers will be treated in the same way as all other market participants and effectively banned from naked short selling.

If naked short selling doesn't exist, and it's not a problem, then why the legislation? That is my point.

On November 4, 2008, voters in South Dakota had a ballot initiative—the South Dakota Small Investor Protection Act—to end naked short selling in their state. However, the Securities Industry and Financial Markets Association of Washington and New York said they would take legal action if the measure passed. The initiative was defeated by the voters subsequently.[19]

The SEC's enforcement actions taken and the initiatives surrounding the abuses of naked short selling directly affect market-makers and financial entities. We only make brief mention of it here so that you are aware of it.

International stock exchanges typically either partially or fully restrict the practice of naked shorting. These include the Australia Securities Exchange, India, the Netherland's Euronext

---

18   sec.gov
19   wikipedia.org/wiki/naked_short_selling

Amsterdam, Japan's Tokyo Stock Exchange, Switzerland's SWX Swiss Exchange, and the Singapore Exchange.

Over the last few years, the SEC has fined many companies for their involvement in illegal naked shorting. In December 2006, the SEC sued Gryphon Partners, a hedge fund for insider trading and naked shorting involving PIPE's in the unregistered stock of thirty-five companies. PIPE's—private investments in public equities—are used by companies to fund themselves. The naked shorting took place in Canada, where it was legal at the time.

In March 2007, Goldman Sachs was fined $2 million by the SEC for allowing customers to illegally short prior to secondary public offerings.[20]

In June 2007, executives at Universal Express claimed naked shorting of its stock. Universal Express claimed that 6,000 small companies had been put out of business by naked shorting, which the company claimed "the SEC has ignored and condoned."[21]

Another entity called the Depository Trust and Clearing Corporation (DTCC) has been criticized for its approach to naked short selling. The DTCC was set up in the late nineties basically to provide clearing, settlement, and information services for all market transactions that occur in the United States.

The DTCC has been sued with regard to its alleged participation in naked short selling. Critics state that the DTCC has been too secretive with information about where naked shorting is taking place. Many lawsuits have been filed against the DTCC over the past few years regarding naked shorting and DTCC's involvement.

A Government Accountability Office study released in June 2009 found that recent SEC rules had apparently reduced abusive

---

20 wikipedia.org/wiki/naked_short_selling
21 wikipedia.org/wiki/naked_short_selling

short selling, but that the SEC needed to give clearer guidance to the brokerage industry.[22]

The *Los Angeles Times* called the practice of naked short selling "hard to defend," and stated that it was past time the SEC become active in addressing market manipulation.[23]

In July 2008, Frank Ahrens of the *Washington Post*, described naked shorting as "far more dangerous than sexy. It's a frenetic shadow work of postponed promises, borrowed time, obscured paperwork, and nail-biting price-watching usually compressed into a few high-tension days swirling around the decline of a company."

The biggest bankruptcy in United States history might have been avoided had this practice been prevented.

In 2008, as Lehman Brothers struggled to survive, 32.8 million shares were sold short and not delivered to buyers on time as of September 11, according to Bloomberg and the SEC. That was more than a fifty-seven-fold increase over the prior year's peak of 567,518 failed trades on July 30! On September 17, two days after Lehman filed for bankruptcy, the number of failed trades climbed to 49.7 million![24] Oliver Stone's movie *Wall Street* didn't exactly mention any of this!

The SEC has linked so-called fails to deliver to naked short selling, which is a strategy that is used to manipulate stocks and markets. By definition, a fail to deliver trade is a trade that doesn't settle within three days like normal trades.

"We had another word for this in Brooklyn," said former SEC chairman Harvey Pitt. "The word was fraud."

What you need to understand is that the trading patterns as evidenced by 2008 SEC data showed naked shorting contributed

---

22 wikipedia.org/wiki/naked_short_selling
23 wikipedia.org/wiki/naked_short_selling
24 Bloomberg

to the fall of Lehman Brothers and Bear Stearns. Hundreds of thousands of failed trades appeared in the data.

"Abusive short selling amounts to gasoline on the fire for distressed stocks and distressed markets," stated United States Senator Ted Kaufman, a Delaware democrat.

Failed trades correlate with drops in share value—enough to account for 30 to 70 percent of the declines in Bear Stearns, Lehman, and other stocks in 2008, according to Suzanne Trimbath, a trade-settlement expert and president of STP Advisory Services, an Omaha, Nebraska-based consulting firm.

Failing to deliver is almost as if someone is just issuing new shares in a company without their permission. It increases the number of shares circulating in the market, which devalues the stock. It's very similar to our government printing more money. What do you think happens to our currency? Has our currency gone up or down in value in the past couple of years? I think you get the picture.

Former Lehman Brothers CEO Richard Fuld said that a host of factors, including a crisis of confidence and naked short selling attacks followed by false rumors contributed to both the collapse of Bear Stearns and Lehman Brothers.[25]

Let's examine this further for some more insight.

There were massive amounts of naked short selling coming from Dubai and London which as you know, destroyed both Bear Stearns and Lehman Brothers stock. What is really interesting to note is the date of the massive amounts of short selling. September 11, 2008, that's right, 9/11/2008. Coincidental date? I think not.

In fact, the Pentagon hired Kevin Freeman to investigate and write a report on financial terrorism.

Freeman describes these attacks in three main phases in his 2009 report:

---

25 NY CNN/Money.com, Oct 6, 2008

"The first phase was a speculative run-up in oil prices that generated as much as $2 trillion of excess wealth for oil producing nations, filling the coffers of Sovereign Wealth Funds, especially those that follow Sharia Compliant Finance. The rapid run up in oil prices made the value of OPEC oil in the ground roughly $137 trillion (based on $125 barrel oil) virtually equal to the value of all the other world financial assets including every share of stock, bond, every private company, all government and corporate debt, and the entire world's bank deposits.

The second phase appears to have begun in 2008 with a series of bear raids targeting US financial services firms that appeared to be systemically significant. An initial bear raid against Bear Stearns was successful in forcing the firm to near bankruptcy. It was acquired by JP Morgan for pennies on the dollar. The attacks continued until the outright failure of Lehman Brothers. This created a system wide crisis, caused the collapse of the credit markets, and nearly collapsed the global financial system. The bear raids were perpetrated by naked short selling and manipulation of credit default swaps, both of which were virtually unregulated. What can be demonstrated, however, is that two relatively small broker dealers emerged virtually overnight to trade trillions of dollars worth of US blue chip companies. They are the number one traders in all financial companies that collapsed or are now financially supported by the US government. Trading by the firms has grown exponentially while the markets have lost trillions of dollars in value.

The risk of a Phase Three has quickly emerged, suggesting a potential direct economic attack on the US Treasury and US dollar. Such an event has already been discussed by finance ministers in major emerging market nations such as China and Russia as well as Iran and the Arab states. A focused effort to collapse the dollar by dumping Treasury bonds has grave implications including the possibility of a downgrading of US debt forcing rapidly rising interest rates and a collapse of the American economy. In short, a bear raid against the US financial system remains possible and may even be likely."[26]

Freeman's report substantiates naked short selling and sheds light to the manipulation of the financial markets which hurt some companies, and destroyed others not to mention investors along the way. There you have it.

According to NYSE Regulation Inc, (the regulatory arm of the NYSE) four exchange member firms were fined for naked shorting. JP Morgan Securities Inc. paid the highest penalty— $400,000—as part of an agreement in which the firm neither admitted nor denied guilt.

The Financial Industry Regulatory Authority (FINRA) announced that they had fined UBS Securities $12 million dollars for failing to properly supervise short sales of securities.

FINRA officials say that the violations resulted in millions of short-sale orders being incorrectly marked and/or placed to the market without proof that the securities could be borrowed and delivered.

The bottom line: Now you know what naked shorting or naked short selling is, and you know that it has occurred and has helped destroy many, many companies. You now know how naked shorting affects markets and can negatively impact your own investments unless you avoid it. Just remember that when you see a stock in any company trade excessive volume (that is more volume than in the float or outstanding for that matter) to the downside on a daily basis, sell if you own it, and do not buy any more just because you think it looks cheap or is a good value.

---

26 Washington Times, March 1, 2011

What Causes Bubbles to Burst?

Now that you have a better understanding of the Federal Reserve and the power that they wield, let's look at some actual bubbles that occurred and what really happened.

First, in the late 1990's, the markets were flying. Technology and Internet companies were making billionaires virtually overnight. Interest rates were low, and investors were clamoring to buy the next Internet IPO, and pushing stock prices to levels never before seen. These excessively high stock prices led to the technology bubble. Tremendous wealth was made in this bubble prior to 2000.

So then what caused the bubble to burst? Why did the market sell off so abruptly in 2000? Well, to find the answers, we have to look no further then the central bank. You will find out how the bubble burst, but you won't find out necessarily why, unless you use your own cognitive thinking and deductive reasoning.

Let's look and see what the FED did. The Central Bank Chairman Alan Greenspan raised interest rates 7 times in 2000, during the very last year of Bill Clinton's presidency. Do you think then President Clinton would want to leave his last year in office with a rapidly declining stock market and an economy going into recession? The President could not stop the FED from raising interest rates. Why not? I think you know the reason now.

So why did the FED do what they did? Well, think about it for a second…with great wealth comes power, and these billionaires could have been a potential threat to the central bankers. Plain and simple. I know many of you reading this think this is so ridiculous and just plain stupid. Not so fast. When you look at history, and understand how the central banks operate, I believe you too will come to the same logical conclusion. My hope is that your eyes have been opened and your mind illuminated to what really is going on, not only in our own financial system but in our world.

So, we had the tech bubble burst by rising interest rates. When interest rates rise, money leaves the stock market and goes elsewhere, predominantly to interest bearing investments. Great destruction of wealth by the sheer manipulation of interest rates. It's really that simple. Think about it. No one should have the ability to set or control interest rates. If we had a truly free market, the market would set interest rates.

Let's look at the recent housing market that has declined so massively. Well, there were many people again making a lot of money. It seemed that everyone was buying and selling homes. Big money was being made by many people. So guess what… here they come…the bubble police… Here comes the FED. And guess what they did? Raised interest rates naturally. In fact, the FED raised interest rates 17 times in a row! That's right, 17 times without even a pause to let the housing market and economy absorb the impact. Nope, total wealth destruction for real estate investors, real estate developers, and all US homeowners.

I was on the radio in 2005 and 2006 talking about this, and

pleading that the FED needed to stop raising interest rates. All to no avail of course. The point is I was trying to educate and get as many people to know what was going on and that this was not going to be a good thing by any means. So, the housing bubble burst, started by the FED raising interest rates. But who was listening then? I just hope that this time, the words are not in vain.

Do you get the picture now?

What Drives the Stock Market?

As an investor, you need to know how the Fed influences our financial markets, especially with respect to the bond and stock market. How many times have we heard that earnings drive stocks and investor psychology or consumer sentiment? This is all true—to an extent.

I am going to explain what really drives the stock and bond market. Pay particular attention here, because once you understand what the Fed is doing, you will know what the *smart money* is doing. And then invest accordingly. The Fed influences our market through open market operations.

This is how it essentially works. When the government is short of money, the Treasury issues bonds and delivers them to bond dealers, which auction them off. When the Fed wants to expand the money supply, it steps in and buys bonds from these dealers with newly issued dollars acquired by the Fed for the cost of writing them into an account on a computer screen. The bonds then become the "reserves" that the banks use to back their loans.

This is where the term "fractional reserve banking" comes into play. The same reserves are lent as much as ten times over, further expanding the money supply and the amount of interest that the banks can make. The basic reserve requirement set by the Fed is 10 percent. That means that a bank with $100,000 in reserves can lend out 10 times the amount or $1 million. Not a bad way to make money now—is it?

In essence, the Fed is either buying or selling bonds, i.e. Treasuries. If the Fed is buying paper, which is what they have been doing now through QE3 and so forth, then the Fed is injecting massive amounts of liquidity in the markets. Why? Because they are buying paper from the banks and financial institutions that then have excess cash to put into the stock market, which drives stock prices higher.

Liquidity ultimately drives the stock market.

That is why when the announcement came in November 2010 that the Fed is going to buy $600 billion worth of Treasuries, the stock market traded substantially higher.

Conversely, if the Fed wants the stock market lower, they will sell Treasuries, which the banks and financial institutions are required to buy. This means that they have to raise cash from selling stocks, which drives the stock market lower.

What is so bothersome today is how Wall Street and the government are so intertwined. Why is this so troubling with respect to the Fed buying all this government paper? Because the Fed is buying the paper from Goldman Sachs, Goldman Sachs can go into the market and start bidding or buying paper and then mark it up by who knows how much to the Fed. On a $600-billion-transaction, the commissions could be in the billions. Not bad, right?

The central bank as well as all central banks should be

transparent. The only reason for secrecy is to hide something. An efficient market based system working in the public's best interest would have nothing to hide and its administrators nothing to fear. Obviously, this is not what we have today.

Stocks today trade in decimals—thanks to a complete pricing makeover after many complaints by investors over the years because of the spreads that existed in stocks. Stocks used to trade in fractions, and the difference between the bid and ask (what you would get if you bought and sold) is called the spread. The commissions from the amount of the spread on many stocks could be fairly significant in many situations.

Since the bond market has not had the same pricing makeover, bonds still trade in fractions. Most unsuspecting investors believe that they are buying bonds commission free, which is definitely not the case because of the fact that bonds still trade in fractions. This means that you can buy a bond today and if you want to immediately sell it, chances are because of the fact that the bond was marked up to you, you can't get back what you just paid for the bond. The commissions are built in to the price of the bond that brokers sell to the investing public. Unlike with stocks, they have no clue how much the broker made on the deal.

This is another subject that we will not discuss here because we want to focus on the ***smart money*** and how it translates to making money. You don't typically invest in bonds to make money. The wealthiest investors in the world didn't get there by buying bonds.

Let's get back to the Fed buying paper from Goldman Sachs. When we say the Fed is buying Treasuries, you know by now that we are referring specifically to the New York Fed. However, why Goldman? It just so happens that the current president of the New

York Fed is William C. Dudley. Guess where Mr. Dudley used to work? He was a former managing director at Goldman Sachs. How convenient, huh? Does anyone see a conflict? Can you see the ties between the government and Wall Street?

Now you know that liquidity is what really drives the stock market. You also should understand that all the hype you hear about hyperinflation may or may not happen. The key is to watch what the central banks are doing. We all know they are printing money, typically leading to higher prices and inflation. Remember that the same people causing inflation can stop it by ceasing the printing of money, selling Treasuries—thus decreasing liquidity, forcing banks to raise reserves—and raising interest rates. This is exactly what caused deflation from 1929–1939.

Hyperinflation can occur when a government cannot borrow any more money because its debt is so great that investors believe they will never be paid back with close to the same purchasing power. As a result of this lack of confidence in the markets, a government is forced to print money to meet its obligations. This undermines its own currency, which can lead to a frenzied collapse. Does this sound familiar?

Remember, hyperinflation is only caused by governments and central banks.

WHY FOLLOW SMART MONEY?

The case has been made just why it's so important to disregard all the financial pornography that exists today. We call it pornography because there is so much of it around—and it can become so addicting. Financial pornography includes, but is not limited to financial magazines, newspapers, radio, television, trading software, the Internet, newsletters, research reports, brokers, analysts, and friends. We have never had so much information available to us.

We all know the old adage "Knowledge is power." Let's take it one step further. "Accurate knowledge is power." What we mean by this will be discussed in great detail in the accompanying pages, but understand that there has never been so much information passing through so many channels at such lightning speed.

We will examine why you need to protect yourself—and how to protect yourself—from becoming infected and addicted to these sources of information and why we consider them to be financial pornography.

First we will look at financial magazines. There are many problems with the written media. Many financial magazines do not offer objective, unbiased research. Quite simply, many of the articles are paid for by companies, institutions, or individuals for their gain—not yours or mine. Sometimes there are people that receive the information before they hit the newsstands. And if that's not enough, the information is written for the masses. We don't want what's for the masses because we all know that the masses or general public tend to be like sheep—and sheep get led to the slaughter.

In the April/May 2008 issue, *Worth* magazine said, "Emerging markets are now the global investors' safe haven of choice." Guess what happened? Emerging market stocks got creamed in the second half of 2008.

On July 14, 2008, *Barron's* said, "Home prices are about to bottom." Oh really? Home price declines actually accelerated so much that new records were broken in the second half of the year.

Most television shows again are for the masses. Advertisers can certainly influence the shows, but sometimes the person or persons on the show have their own agenda. Having said that, we must note in all fairness, that the SEC is working on requiring more disclosure on recommendations that are made. The stock jockeys that used to move stocks on the business channels are no more. Analysts do appear everyday and some have more influence than others. Can you find a good idea now and then? Of course you can. Can you find a lot more non-sense and conflicting views? Absolutely.

Just be aware that the mainstream mass media is very biased and sometimes not as objective as you might think. How many times have we heard about all the money that the oil companies make like Exxon, and Chevron here in the US? Do you realize that they are not even in the top five of all the oil companies in the world? So if you are going to attack and complain about the US companies making money, be accurate and give a complete picture of the industry. Why not mention that the US government takes more of the oil companies' profits than they themselves do. I mean come on...How many people realize this? I know they make a lot, but so do many other companies in many different industries. The point here is clearly the recent attack on the oil companies was deliberate and biased. And don't think for a minute that I am defending the oil companies for a second. I am only pointing out an example of how misleading, biased, self serving, the mass media can be.

Many trading software programs are available today—probably more than ever before. Each one claims that it has the highest success rate and will make you more money. Our experience is that this is simply not the case. Logic dictates that if someone truly developed trading software that could guarantee winning trades, everyone would probably use it. Moreover, if there was trading software that was truly good, the chances are good that we would never know about it—and probably would not want to pay the price for it—especially if it's worth its weight in gold. By the time we could afford it, it would no longer be effective because so many others would already be using it.

We all know that the Internet has changed how we get information and the way we do business. It has also changed *how* we invest. You have to be careful with the Internet because there is so much information literally at your fingertips. You can find reliable, accurate information, but only from credible, legitimate sources and websites. There are so many places to get inaccurate, worthless opinions. You have no idea who is posting comments on the blogs that you read. Not only that, but you don't know the motive or angle behind their comments. Once in a while you may get lucky by finding a genuine, honest person that is making comments to help you. Good luck.

Today there are so many newsletters that promise returns, the next super stock, or whatever. Again, if the person writing the newsletter really made good recommendations and they all continuously worked, then why would they be in the business of trying to get you and me to buy their newsletter?

There are some excellent newsletters out there, but there isn't one that delivers consistent results on each and every one of its recommendations. I should know something about this since I was a newsletter publisher years ago. I too had one or two great years of returns based on my recommendations, but that was short lived. However, on occasion you may discover a good idea here or there. But you will waste a lot of time and money. If you have both, then as Stallone said to Clubber Lang in *Rocky III*, "Go for it!"

We are all aware of the negative publicity over the past decade regarding Wall Street analysts and the biased research and recommendations over the Internet and technology stocks. Wall Street has come a long way in cleaning up the unbiased analysis, but they still play a lot of games that are designed to benefit the brokerage firm or institutional investor—not you and me.

And what do you do, when a major brokerage firm or analyst issues research that you can't make heads or tails out of. This is where the research recommendation makes no sense or is so confusing that it is mind boggling. There are literally so many examples that you will find when you do your own research. Here is one such example. In March 2011, Credit Suisse Bank took Research in Motion (RIMM) off of its focus list. The stock traded down naturally for the day and closed at $54.75. The reason they gave was that they see the company losing market share, which could weigh on margins. This sounds certainly reasonable. However, they maintained an outperform rating, and an $85 price target! For a stock to go from $54.75 to $85 is not a bad return, more than 50%!. If you are taking a stock off of your focus list, wouldn't it be logical based on the reasons given for doing so, that you would lower your rating and price target on the stock? I mean come on.

Or how about this. April 12, 2011, Goldman Sachs comes out and makes major headlines by saying to sell oil. Their opinion stated that they felt oil put in a top, and that lower oil prices are coming, and that investors should sell their oil stocks. Ok, you might think that was a pretty gutsy call. Well, the market sold off that day, with major declines in all the oil related equities. I mean that is what you would expect. Right?

The next day, I mean the very next day, Bank of America aka Merrill Lynch states the exact opposite. They put a buy on oil, with prognostications of oil prices significantly higher by the third quarter. So naturally the oil stocks traded up that day as well as the overall market. Now there is no telling how much money was lost by investors who heard through the media or from their broker about Goldman's bold call. What does one do? I mean someone is going to be right and someone is going to be wrong. Both firms are at the exact polar opposite in terms of their feelings regarding the price of oil. This is the kind of financial pornography, noise, and crazy Wall St analysis that you want to avoid at all cost. It is not always easy to do, but you can get crazy here with trying to figure out what to do when you listen to what is made for the masses.

Check this out. Diane Garrick, who was the investment strategist for Invesco stated on March 9, 2009, that "There's a long way to go" before the market or economy bottoms. I do believe the market bottomed shortly thereafter.

On April 28, 2003, the Associated Press reported, "Securities regulators today announced a settlement that will cost ten big Wall Street firms $1.4 billion and require reforms to resolve allegations that they issue biased stock ratings to lure investment banking business."[27]

This is another area that you have to be careful. Brokerage firms will bring a company public and then issue research, which is usually positive on the company. So, is the research really unbiased? How can it be, if the brokerage firm made money off of the company going public? So, watch for this.

More recently, Crocs Inc. (CROX) on October 18, 2011 missed earnings and the stock plummeted over $10 a share or over 40%. DA Davidson downgraded the stock from a buy to a hold. Ok, that sounds normal and understandable. Hold on a second, Standpoint Research upgrades the stock from hold to buy, the very same day!!!! Two conflicting, precisely opposite opinions. I mean the analysts are all reading the exact same numbers from the company and come up with completely opposite opinions. What does one do as an investor? Someone is right, and someone is wrong. Do you flip a coin? I mean what does the average investor do in a situation like this?

Need we say more? And this isn't just commonplace with just the large firms. This occurs with small, mid size, as well as the large investment firms.

Perhaps nothing has as far reaching effects and influence on today's investor as the financial channels on television. We

---

27   Associated Press

understand that no one is perfect—and we give the benefit of the doubt that the host is really trying to help us as investors. However, if one were to look back at the stock selections and guidance, perhaps we would have been better off watching reruns of *The Honeymooners*.

On August 28, 2008, Larry Kudlow said, "With the U.S. dollar up and oil down and businesses investing, I think Goldilocks (economy) is back in business."[28] That was just weeks before the market began it's nearly 3,000-point drop with Lehman going under. These kinds of quotes are common if one were to replay the prior shows.

Jim Cramer from CNBC's *Mad Money* said, "The market will not revisit the panicked lows it hit on July 15 (2008) ... Bye-bye, bear market. Say hello to the bull, and don't let the door hit you on the way out."[29] This was just before the Dow fell another 3,400 points. Replay shows for his top stock picks and you'll understand just how vulnerable your portfolio would have been. Whether it's Cramer or someone else talking, the same can be said.

Now Mr. Cramer tries to help investors to the best of his ability. In all fairness, it is very difficult to know everything about every stock. After all, there are more than 25,000 publicly traded companies. When you make as many recommendations as he makes, you are bound to get some right and some wrong. His show is meant to be both educational and entertaining, which is not easy to do and he does it better than anyone.

Brokers are another area that you need to be aware of. The vast majority of brokers and financial advisors try to do the best job they can for you. The problem is that many are inexperienced

---

28 CNBC
29 CNBC

and have inaccurate information—or are just plain deceived by their firm's research.

The other problem that you need to be aware of is that if you have an account at a brokerage firm, it can be difficult for the broker to truly offer what is best for you because not every product is available at every firm. Some products are proprietary, and the brokerage firms like their brokers selling certain programs and products. The larger brokerage firms and wirehouses such as Merrill Lynch started losing many brokers to independent firms years ago, many for this very reason. To get truly knowledgeable, objective, unbiased research, one needs to speak with a true independent financial advisor—one whose broker-dealer does not offer proprietary products, investment banking, or paid analysts.

On the other discount side of the business, firms such as TD Ameritrade, Fidelity, and Charles Schwab employ brokers that tend to be very young and inexperienced. They are simply company employees—nothing more than order takers. They typically do not have the experience, knowledge, or independent thinking that you can find elsewhere. If they did, they wouldn't be working for a large discount firm. You do not want brokers that take directives from their employer regarding what they recommend. This is definitely not where the *smart money* is.

Last but not least, let's just touch on friends for a minute. We all have friends that are investors just as we are. Sometimes you get a good idea or two that work out. But more often than not—unless your neighbor is a guy like Carlos Slim or Bill Gates—they simply do not. You have heard about how the only good tip is the one you give a waiter—it is so true. I can't begin to tell you how many tips I received over the years that cost me a few cars—and I am not talking about Smart cars! Even brokers get tips that simply do not pan out. I even had tips from people that I considered to be "in the know." However, it always seemed as if I was on the wrong side. The problem is that you don't know who is on the other side of the stock that you are buying unless it's a real blue chip company—and even then you need to be somewhat careful.

The same thought process with regard to ignoring the financial media can be used in life. Just as the financial media can be used by people to take your money and adversely impact your financial wellbeing, so too can the mass media. The mass media does not present objectively and the information that the masses receive is controlled—as it is in many other countries as well. To get the full story or a different perspective, you have to look to independent news sources. You can use www.realnews.com, www.rawstory.com, www.truthout.org , and www.guardiannews.com.

These will provide plenty of information that you can access to get the information you need.

It's important that we share this with you because this is not just about being smart with your investing, but also with regard to what really is going on in our world. You will find that this philosophy will carry over and permeate other areas of your life.

How Smart Money Works

Smart money—as we have mentioned—is big money and quiet money. We have found that there are several ways to identify what the **smart money** is doing. It's not always easy, but we will explain our methodologies and where we look. Basically you just have to look—if you want to be successful investing and in life.

We have mentioned how important it is to track the insiders. As you know by now, we are not talking about insider trading, which is the act of trading on material non-public information. This is what happened to Bud Fox and Gordon Gekko in the movie "Wall Street."

The people who place the trades are not the only ones guilty of insider trading. Anyone "tipping" an outsider with material non-public information can be found guilty as well. The SEC uses the "Dirks Test" to determine if an insider gave a tip illegally. The test states that if a tipster breaches his or her trust with the company and understands that this was a breach, he or she is liable for insider trading.[30]

---

30 sec.gov

We are talking about following the insiders. What is an insider? According to the SEC, an insider is a corporate officer or director of a company or anyone that owns 10 percent or more of the shares outstanding. Institutions buy a lot of stock. However, they tend to be a little more long-term in their outlook.

We do not care about a corporate secretary buying a few shares—or for that matter any purchase in someone's 401(k)—that is routine. It has been our experience to follow the big money—that is when the insiders are buying millions of dollars worth of stock. There is no better buy signal that you can get that is better than insider buying. Insiders tend to be investors and not traders. They tend to buy stock in the company when they feel it is undervalued and timely, and sell when they believe it's expensive.

We mainly track and focus on five people: the company's president, chief executive officer, chief financial officer, chief operating officer, and chairman of the board. When we see insider purchases in the millions of dollars by one or more of these people, we pay particular attention. And so should you.

This book focuses on the United States because our markets tend to be more regulated than other markets—and because of the fraudulent practices that can occur in other markets where rules and regulations are not commonplace or enforced. A few years ago in France, the insiders of Airbus sold massive amounts of shares just before the stock massively declined when the company announced problems and delays with the new A380.

Another market of interest is Brazil. There is a long tradition of a culture of corruption. And we have found that the higher the corruption level in a country, the more intense insider trading practices in that country tend to be. And the actual level of enforcement appears to need a much greater emphasis.

It is hard enough to make money in the United States of America in a so called free market system with regulatory bodies governing and safeguarding the markets from all sorts of illegal and criminal activity. So, we will just stay focused on the US markets for now.

No one invests to lose money. Insiders know their industry better than any outside analyst and are the first to be aware of changes inside their company or in their sector that may lead to stock price gains. Following their purchases will uncover opportunities that you may otherwise have been unaware of. Conversely, when we see massive selling in a company by insiders, we pay particular attention—and so should you.

Take for example World Online. The company went public in 1999. CEO Nina Brink sold out her entire position to a hedge fund in San Francisco. By the way, this was the largest IPO in the Netherlands at the time, and turned out to be a scam. The story didn't really make headlines here in the US, but the Netherlands Supreme Court ruled that the company and Goldman Sachs misled investors. Nina Brink knew it, and sold out while she could.

Numerous examples abound here in the US with WorldCom and Enron. If employees at WorldCom and Enron along with investors for that matter had paid attention to the massive insider selling by corporate executives, they too could have sold and saved their retirements and investment portfolios.

The SEC prohibits insiders from taking profits on shares held less than six months. This means that insiders must invest their money with an eye to the long-term prospects of the company.

If these insiders are investing with a six-month horizon, we can be reasonably confident that the stock price will be higher in six months than it is today. However, keep in mind that not every insider purchasing activity results in a higher stock price. After all, insiders are human and humans make mistakes in their judgment—not to mention the possibility of unforeseen events or acts of God. That is why it is so important to look for multiple, large purchases by the five key executives that we mentioned. In general, insiders are the most informed people when it comes to investing in their own companies.

We haven't mentioned institutional buying. Sometimes you will see millions upon millions of dollars going into a particular stock or ETF, and you begin salivating at the possibility that maybe you just found something. Well, hold on because you will find where some fund, holding co., or corporation is buying huge amounts of stock. What does this mean? Is this good? What should you do with this information? This is certainly interesting, and perhaps worth looking into. Suppose you find some unknown corporation or entity buying huge amounts of stock in XYZ Company. Well, try to find out who is behind the corporation buying the stock. Have they just been accumulating stock periodically over the past 3 or 10 years? And are they just buying to employ cash or for a specific reason?

There are only really two ideal scenarios to pay attention to when it comes to institutional buying. Sometimes, you will find out that there is a huge insider or extremely wealthy individual that is buying stock through his holding co, entity or corporation. This is done quite frequently for various reasons. For example, you will find the name, Tracinda Corp. which owns huge amounts of shares in a number of companies. Well, upon further investigation, it just so happens that Tracinda is Carl Icahn's. Here is definitely an example of "**smart money**", and obviously worth paying attention to. This is the first ideal scenario.

On the other hand, you might find a mutual fund buying huge amounts of shares. They are buying not because they necessarily "know" something, as much as they are having to file their purchases because they are an insider and they own 10% or more of the outstanding shares in the company. This kind of buying or filing by an institution is not as important.

What if you find one very successful, large hedge fund or a number of hedge funds that are buying shares in XYZ company? Jackpot. This is the other ideal scenario that you want to be able to find in institutional buying.

NOT ALL INSIDERS ARE EQUAL

There have been some academic studies regarding which insiders have had more success than others. However, they haven't been as thorough and as complete as we would like to see. Obviously, one company may have a CEO and no president, while another may have both roles filled by the same person. We all know that every company has a unique corporate culture.

There was one study that we will point out to you regarding the marketing officer. A study was done with 472 different individuals (each with the title as marketing officer) that purchased stock between 2004 and June of 2009. If you had bought every time they bought stock and evaluated your portfolio at the end of every quarter between 2004 and June 2009, your entire portfolio would have dipped 1.3 percent below its purchase price once, and would have risen to a maximum of 557.72 percent above its purchase price once.[31] This is fairly significant data, but our experience leads us to follow not any one particular insider.

If you find huge insider buying in a company, don't go out and just buy the stock. You might also want to look and see if

---

31 e-viaminvest.com

the insiders have any kind of prior track record. Obviously, if someone has a proven track record of consistently making money on their purchases, they will likely make money on their future purchases as well.

Sometimes you will find an insider buying stock simply because the company's corporate bylaws require its officers and/or directors to buy stock. This you want to pay no attention to. Also avoid falling prey to small insider buying that unfortunately occurs when they are trying to entice buying in the marketplace. On the other hand, if you find a corporate officer on a $100,000 salary, and he is buying $50,000 or more of their stock, pay attention. It's not really big money as we are focused on, but sometimes you may find a unique situation such as this—and you will need to pay attention.

A director of a company that is making $40 million and invests $700,000 isn't as important as another officer that invests a majority of his annual salary. The size of the purchases relative to their salaries lets you know how confident they feel regarding their investment. Don't assume that a $50,000 investment means nothing compared to a million-dollar investment. It's all relative. Do your research carefully. After all, it's your money and investing is a serious game.

The single most important buy signal that you can get is insider buying. But perhaps the most important reason to follow the insiders is because the research supports doing so. Nejat Seyhun, a professor and researcher in the field of insider buying at the University of Michigan, found that when executives bought shares in their own companies, the stock tended to outperform the total market by 8.9 percent over the next twelve months. Conversely, when they sold shares, the stock underperformed the market by 5.4 percent.

Professor Seyhun completed this study based on every

insider buy and sell from 1985–2005. This research should not be taken lightly or with a grain of salt. It is the most thorough research on insider buying to date and the numbers are decidedly conclusive.[32]

Historical statistics show that, in general, insiders have been good market timers. They have been heavy buyers at important market lows and heavy sellers at or near market tops. You can look as far back as the 1970s. In 1974, there was a tremendous amount of insider buying, and then huge sellers in 1976 (the Dow hit 1,026). In early 1978, the Dow hit a low of 736.75, and again we saw heavy insider buying. Before the November massacre of the same year, we saw heavy insider selling. Are you starting to get the picture? In the spring of 1980, heavy insider buying—followed by heavy insider selling toward the end of 1980.

In late 1981–1982—shortly before the market took off—insiders were also heavy buyers of stocks, but turned to heavy selling near the 1983 top. In 1984 and 1985, they bought heavily just before the market rose. However, in 1987, we did not see heavy insider selling before the market crash in October.

In the 1990s, we saw massive insider buying before the market averages hit all-time highs in 1999. There was massive insider selling before the market averages hit decade-lows. The latest analysis showed massive insider buying occurred in the spring of 2009, which you will see in the following pages. All this was followed by record amount of insider selling in the late summer of 2009.[33]

---

32 getabstract.com
33 en.scientificcomons.org

What Forms Insiders Use

Now that you know what insiders to follow and what kind of activity you want to see before you consider buying, you also need to understand the rules that they must abide by.

Sarbanes–Oxley changed insider transaction reporting from the tenth day of the following month to two days. That means that insiders must report their trades within two business days from their activity. Changes in insider holdings are sent to the SEC electronically as a Form 4 that details a company's insider trades or loans. Insiders are also not allowed to buy and sell stock based on information that has not yet been made available to the public. Otherwise this would be labeled as "insider trading," the kind that is illegal. Insiders are also prohibited from selling their shares within six months.

Insiders are required to file Forms 3, 4, and 5. We are not going to analyze each form, but you need to know basically what each form represents so that when you are doing your research, you know what each form is and what forms you want to read.

The initial filing is Form 3. This is where an insider of an issuer that is registering stock for the first time under Section 12 of the Exchange Act must file this form no later than the effective date of the registration statement. If the issuer is already registered under Section 12, the insider must file a Form 3 within ten days of becoming an officer, director, or beneficial owner.

Changes in ownership are reported on Form 4 and must be reported to the SEC within two business days. Form 4 reveals which insider is trading, whether their trade was a buy or sell, and whether it was an option or open-market purchase.

Insiders that file Form 5 report transactions that should have been reported earlier on a Form 4 or were eligible for deferred reporting. If a form must be filed, it is due forty-five days after the end of the company's fiscal year.

The insider trading rules to submit Forms 3, 4, and 5 not only help prevent illegal insider trading, but they also give us a chance to see how management and the insiders view their companies.

We follow and look at Form 4 filings simply because we want to know who is buying and selling. Yes, it's basic, but it's the filings that you want to pay attention to and follow. Most of the filings that you will come across will be Form 4 filings.

Why isn't everyone following insiders? The short answer is that, until very recently, no one could. The problem was that for nearly seventy years, insiders didn't have to report their trades until ten days after the end of the month in which they occurred. Insiders that traded shares at the beginning of a month could have waited as long as forty days before reporting their trades. At that point, the information carried limited value to outside investors.

Insiders at Work

Let's take a look at a few insider buys of some common—and not-so-common—names along with resulting stock prices:

- Systemax Inc. (SYX) soared 70 percent in several weeks after insiders bought in March 2008.
- Gold Inc. (FCX) shot up more than 90 percent in six months after insiders bought $62 million worth of stock in the first quarter of 2007.
- Capstead Mortgage Corp. (CMO) soared 100 percent after insiders bought stock in 2006 and 2007.
- American Pacific Corp (APFC) soared more than 100 percent after insiders purchased in the first half of 2006.
- Sandridge Energy Inc. (SD) soared more than 100 percent in just a few months after huge insider buying in early 2008.
- Bank of America (BAC) saw insider buying in February and March of 2009 and then soared over 700 percent in just five months!
- Las Vegas Sands (LVS) had over 25 million shares

purchased in the end of March 2009 at approximately $3 per share. And in just a year and a half, the stock hit over $55 a share, more than 1,800 percent! What's more impressive is that the insiders are up over $1 billion! Not bad for a year and a half. And during this time, S&P downgraded the stock with a sell rating! Imagine that.

- Petroquest Energy (PQ) saw insider buying in the spring of 2009 under $1 per share only to soar more than 1,000 percent in ten months!
- Citigroup (C) had insider buying in March of 2009 starting at $1.24 a share only to be followed up by more insider buying as high as $4 a share in August. On top of that, Paulson was at it again by snapping up millions of shares. At the end of August 2009, the stock was up over $5 a share!

However, six months later, the stock pulled back to $3 a share in early 2010 when the government bought billions of stock at $3.25. If you had known this, what should you have been doing? What is the risk at $3 a share? This is why having timely, accurate information is critical to your success.

Citigroup had a number of buying signals. Not only insider buying, but our definition of big money, **smart money** (Paulson), and the United States government. This is about as good as it gets!

What about Warren Buffett buying Goldman Sachs in the fall of 2008 in the low $130's, only to see his investment drop by over 50 percent in a couple of months, before soaring in the spring of 2010 to over $190 a share!

We will examine a few other cases of a couple of companies

you may and may not be familiar with, and you will see what kinds of returns are possible when you identify strong insider buying.

The first classic case is a company called Kirkland (KIRK). On September 22, 2008, a total of five different insiders purchased stock at $1.95 a share. One of the insiders, Carl Kirkland, actually purchased more than 3.4 million shares! Guess where the stock went? In less than a year, the stock hit over $14, more than 700-percent appreciation or more than seven times your money. Not a bad return, right? This is a classic case because everything that you could want in a potential **smart money** investment is here: a decent number of insiders buying stock and one key insider (big money) purchasing a large amount of stock.

Another classic case is MBIA (MBI). The stock was in the news in late 2008 and early 2009. In late February/March 2009, we noticed over $42 million go into the stock in more than twenty different purchases ranging from $2–$3.59 a share. Just five months later, the stock was trading close to $9 a share. And during the next six months, MBI traded down to just above $3 a share. And then we saw more insider purchases around $5 a share. By October of 2010, the stock jumped to over $13 a share, more than a 400-percent move!

The point is that sometimes *smart money* can look as if it is wrong in the short- or near-term, but long-term is where you can make significant returns. Again, if you followed the insiders in and they haven't sold, why should you? You may not want to take gains until you see the insiders sell.

The third case is a company called ValueVision (VVTV). This company had fifty-eight insider transactions—that's right, fifty-eight!—with stock purchases as low as 28 cents and as high as $1.99 in February and March of 2009. In just five months, the stock was above $4 a share! Returns ranging from 200 percent to 2,000 percent or twenty times your money—now that's what we call **smart money** at work.

Another example is going to hurt to read. Why do I say that? Because in March 2010, Felcor Lodging (FCH) had more than sixty insider buys! That's right—more than sixty buys as low as $3 a share and up to $5 a share. The next month, the stock hit over $9 a share! In one month, gains as much as 300 percent! How many shares did you own?

I think you understand now the gains possible by following the **smart money**. The gains can be rather incredible. You don't have to worry about reading a balance sheet, analyzing ratios, number crunching, research, analysts' opinions, or your broker's or financial advisor's opinion.

That's ***smart money***.

In terms of whether to pay attention to insider buys and sells, the answer is easy. Pay more attention to buys.

> *Insiders might sell their shares for many reasons, but they buy for only one: they think the price will rise.*
> —Peter Lynch

However, you need to take note when you see insider selling, particularly if it's en masse. If you see a number of insiders selling massive amounts of shares—pay attention. That should raise a red flag. *Avoid* the stock.

The insiders at Enron sold 1.1 billion shares in the twelve months leading up to the company's bankruptcy filing. If you saw more than a billion shares being sold by insiders, do you think that maybe you should have sold a few shares? Hello? If the shareholders and all the employees of Enron had seen this, think about how many people could have saved themselves from financial loss and ruin.

The key is to understand that there are typically about fifteen shares sold by insiders for every share bought. Most investors are unaware of this fact and panic when they see insider selling. For example, Bill Gates from Microsoft and Larry Ellison from Oracle have been selling millions of shares each and every year. And if you had panicked and either sold or didn't buy these stocks, you would have missed out on some very strong gains. Just follow our ideas and do not worry unless you see massive insider selling—and not just by one or two insiders.

Another common misunderstanding among many investors is the monthly insider buy/sell ratio, published in the financial press and on websites such as Thompson Financial and Trim Tabs. Trim Tabs investment research provides a lot of information concerning what insiders are not only doing, but thinking as well. In August 2009, Trim Tabs reported that selling by corporate insiders in August surged to $6.1 billion, the highest amount since May 2008. The ratio of insider selling to insider buying hit 30.6, the highest level since Trim Tabs began tracking data in 2004.[34] You can infer from data like this that the insiders are sending a clear signal that the market is going to sell off and trade lower.

Many investors believe the market is about to sell off whenever insider selling spikes. Conversely, whenever insider buying is strong, they believe the market is about to rally. These are logical assumptions. However our experience has been that it isn't an accurate indicator as history bears out.

Insiders know a great deal about the companies they run, but remember that they do not know any more than you do about what the broad market is going to do. While massive insider

---

34 TrimTabs.com

buying can be an indication of a market bottom, widespread insider selling is rarely a sign of a market top.

> *It ... was envisioned by Congress that the reported trades by insiders would provide investors with useful information on which to base investment decisions by giving them an idea of the purchases and sales by insiders which may in turn indicate their private opinion as to the prospects of the company.*
> —H.R. Rep. No. 1383, 73rd Congress,
> 2nd Session, article 13, 1934

There you have it. Congress clearly stated that insider information may be useful for investors. Imagine that! Why do you need anything else? You have the government telling you that following insiders is useful! You think? You don't hear them recommending that you listen to an analyst's recommendations or to all the financial promotion and financial press out there. I wonder why.

Now you know why this book is so important in unveiling and detailing a credible methodology and strategy for investing that can have a dramatic impact in your life.

Let's take a look at a sector that has been in the news lately. We all know that the oil and gas industry exploded in 2007 and half of 2008 before imploding. However, there was a lot of insider buying in many stocks in this sector prior to the huge run up in the prices of oil and gas, along with the huge gains made in the stocks. As early as 1998, millions of dollars went into companies such as Baker Hughes (BHI), Apache (APA), Union Pacific Resources (UPR), Pennzoil (PZL), and Miller Exploration (MEXP). Each one of these companies had at least a half dozen different insiders purchasing stock—and one actually had twelve. You not only had a lot of money being invested, but by a lot of people. This is what you want to try to find. We really like to see this combination of many different buyers and lots of money going into the stock. This would be an example of **smart money.**

We talk about how **smart money** is quiet money and big money. Case in point: On February 22, 2007, Whole Foods announced that they agreed to buy rival Wild Oats Market for a 23 percent premium in price to Wild Oats' one month average closing price. Come to find out, billionaire Ronald Burkle—who controls Yucaipa Companies—owned 17 percent of the outstanding shares. Imagine that. Now, if you had followed the best-of-breed philosophy, you would have owned Whole Foods and missed this one entirely.

In early 2005, Sumner Redstone, chairman of Viacom, was steadily buying shares of a company called Midway Games (NYSE: MWY) in the $4–5 range. Within twelve months, Midway hit over $22 a share—not too shabby during a period where the overall markets were either flat or down for the year.

Kirk Kerkorian began buying shares of General Motors (NYSE: GM) in the last half of 2005 in the $20-range and sold in early 2006 at 50 percent higher. It is interesting to note that the analysts and every financial headline were really negative on General Motors, but Kerkorian was buying in size.

In late November 2008—in the midst of tremendous market turmoil and negativity everywhere you looked—the CEO of Best Buy (NYSE: BBY) was quietly buying more than $13 million of his stock. Financial magazines, newspapers, and analysts on radio and television were saying how bad retail was going to be. Headlines everywhere touted dismal holiday sales and most retail stocks were making fifty-two-week lows—if not all-time lows. Yet the CEO of Best Buy was buying his stock. If you had followed the CEO and ignored all the financial pornography, you would have made close to 50 percent on your money in just a few weeks! This is just another example of **smart money** and why our philosophy is so powerful. It will completely change how and why you invest.

And in February and March of 2009, we saw some of the most significant buys we have ever seen. In February, insiders were buying Bank of America stock at $4 and $6 a share. **Smart money** was going into this stock in the midst of record negativity in the financial markets while most investors and citizens were running scared and selling their shares. If you had followed the insiders—or *smart money*—then you would have seen Bank of America trading above $18 a share in less than six months! Not too shabby.

Again, in the midst of tremendous negativity in Las Vegas, the Adelsons were quietly buying more than 25 million shares of Las Vegas Sands (LVS) at around $3 a share in March 2009. Shares of Las Vegas Sands in November of 2010 traded at over $55 a share.

Do you think that you should have bought a few shares too? Do you see just how important this philosophy and strategy is and how it can impact your portfolio and wealth?

In addition to tracking the insider buying that occurs through SEC filings, you also want to pay attention to what certain people are doing. People such as Kirk Kerkorian, Sumner Redstone, Carlos Slim, Sheldon Adelson, Carl Icahn, Warren Buffett, Bill Gates, and the Sheikh of Dubai. And don't forget about the hedge fund managers that have incredible fortitude in managing money. Men such as John Paulson, George Soros, Steve Cohen, and Joel Greenblatt.

We name only a few here, but they are excellent examples.

If you had followed these men over the past few years, you would have found some excellent ideas for your own portfolio and achieved some very significant returns. In addition, we look at where some of the more savvy and successful mutual fund managers are putting their money. It's okay if you don't recognize some of them, but get to know their names and look for others as well. Become familiar as soon as you can and watch where they are placing their bets. You should be able to gain some valuable insight and ideas.

Why you ask? Because when these people invest, its big money—*smart money*. We don't think it's by accident, coincidence, or luck that they continue to increase their net worth and make money on a consistent basis. Keep in mind that when someone invests millions, they probably have completed more research than the average investor, broker, or analyst. These people tend to be well connected and travel in circles that you and I do not. Therefore they come in contact with information that is both *accurate* and *timely*. This is why you want to watch closely what these people are doing with their money.

This doesn't mean that you should automatically do whatever they do, but try to determine if it interests you and is suitable for you. People such as Warren Buffett tend to be longer-term oriented than the average investor. When he buys, we simply don't go out and buy because he is—unless we think that his position may perform well in the short term. This can be the most powerful strategy when you have identified what the *smart money* is doing.

In the fall of 2008, after the Dow dropped below 8,500, Buffett was all over the media with his comments proclaiming that this was "the time to buy" and "cash is trash." Buffett soon began putting money into General Electric and Goldman Sachs, which both subsequently declined as much as 40–75 percent. In February 2009, Buffett sold many of his stocks, including Johnson & Johnson (JNJ), and moved to fixed income. Truth be told, 2009 was Buffett's worst year. In fact, shares of his Berkshire Hathaway dropped more than 60 percent from the highs. Following the *smart money* is the way to go, but it doesn't look so in this case, does it?

You *can* learn from this. First, *smart money* does not panic and is not short-term oriented. Nor does it pay mind to the mass media, which was very negative at the time. Buffett did not sell his shares in GE or Goldman Sachs even though they dropped significantly right after he purchased them. And both stocks traded 100–150 percent higher from their market lows within twelve months. If you follow the *smart money*, don't let short-term market volatility or the mass media spook you.

What else can we learn from this? First of all, no one is perfect. But we think that there is more to this. Why didn't Buffett realize what the hedge funds were doing in 2008 with the naked short selling? And why didn't he know what kind of government legislation was coming down the pike, thus reflecting in a severe downturn in the financial markets? We don't have those answers. However, we do understand that the really big money—the *smart money*—was in the five hedge funds that were doing the naked short selling. Actually, if we all as investors knew that this was happening, we all would have shorted the market and made a lot of money. This is why it's so important to do your research in order to make sure that you know the rules of the game. In other words, you know what the *smart money* is doing.

9/11 AND THE OPTIONS MARKET

When we talk about *smart money*, it does not solely pertain to stocks, but to commodities, real estate, and options. It is a little more difficult to research where the big money is going, but it is still possible. Let's look back at the news for a second. Examining previous news events may give you an idea of what to look for in the future.

Prior to 9/11, there were some interesting trades that took place. If you had been watching the options market, you would have seen some large option trades take place. A September 21 story by the Israeli Herzliya International Policy Institute for Counterterrorism entitled "Black Tuesday: the World's Largest Insider Trading Scam?" documented the following trades connected to the September attacks:

- Between September 6 and 7, The Chicago Board of Options Exchange saw purchases of 4,744 put options on United Airlines. Assuming that these trades represented "insiders" with advance knowledge of the imminent attacks, the trades in these options represented more than $5 million in profits!

- On September 10, there were 4,516 put options on American Airlines bought on the Chicago exchange, compared to 748 calls. As you know, there was no reason for this kind of trading, no news to justify this. If you assume that 4,000 of these option trades represent "insiders," then this could be a gain of about $4 million. We didn't see any similar trading in other airlines on the Chicago exchange in the days leading up to Black Tuesday. I wonder why. You think these people knew what they were doing? You think?

The level of put options purchased was more than six times higher than normal—another example of **smart money**!

- Morgan Stanley Dean Witter & Co., which occupied twenty-two floors of the World Trade Center, saw 2,157 purchases of its October $5 put options bought in three trading days before 9/11. This compares to an average of twenty-seven contracts a day before September 6. After the attacks, the put options generated in excess of $1 million. Same thing with Merrill Lynch & Co. with headquarters near the World Trade Center had 12,215 October $45 put options bought in the four trading days prior to the attacks (a 1,200 percent increase). When trading resumed, the put options generated in excess of $5.5 million in profit!
- October series options for UAL Corp. were purchased in highly unusual volumes three trading days before the terrorist attacks for a total outlay of $2,070—investors bought the option contracts each representing 100 shares, for 90 cents each. (This represents 230,000 shares). The options are now selling at more than $12 each! There are still 2,313 so-called put options outstanding (valued at $2.77 million and representing

231,300 shares), according to the Options Clearinghouse Corp.[35]

Now, by the end of April 2011, silver prices hit close to $50 an oz, gold topped $1,500 an oz, and oil topped $112 a barrel. Prices were moving higher. The mass media continued headlines of soaring commodity prices, pointing the way to higher and higher prices. After a while, you could easily start to believe that these commodities were going to keep going higher. There was after all, plenty of rational reasons to be bullish.

But then cracks began appearing the very first few days in May. In fact, in just four trading days silver, gold, and oil dropped considerably. Silver in particular dropped from near $50 an oz. to $34 in four days! One silver ETF (AGQ) dropped from a high of $382 to just $179 in four days! People that were long silver, and silver futures contracts got wiped out. What took the metal months to achieve in price, gone in a few days!

I mention all this because Carlos Slim sold 96 million oz. of silver and George Soros sold large positions in both gold and silver before this commodities crash.

However, we did not hear about this in the mainstream media until after the fact, and of course the prices of the metal dropped significantly. Short of knowing these men, or their traders/financial advisors, how would you have known something was up and how could you have seen this coming?

You guessed right, from the options market. That's right. The last day of Friday in April, just two days from the start of this massive slide, the put options on the silver ETF traded 22 times its normal volume for that day. Now that was your key. Obviously, some people knew that the price of silver was coming down. This is exactly what you want to look for. Excessive or unusual volume in the options market.

---

35   hereinreality.com

THE LARGEST INSIDER TRADING SCAM EVER

Let's look at a more recent example of big money, quiet money – **smart money**. This one example could have made all of us literally millions of dollars in just a few days with only a few thousand dollars invested. Only a few thousand dollars invested could have returned millions—in just a few days. How? It would have required taking our philosophy and putting it to practice. It would have required you to look at the stock and option trading in a company that was all over the news in March 2008. What took place with this company should never have happened to any company in America.

It all began with one of the most highly regarded and profitable investment banking giants in the United States. The name of the company is Bear Stearns.

Massive—and I do mean massive—amounts of put options were purchased on Bear Stearns stock in early March. The stock closed at $70 a share on March 10. Puts with strike prices as low as $20 and $22.50 were being bought in massive amounts.[36] It

---

36 bloggingstocks.com, Reuters – Aug 11, 2008

was an extremely risky bet—almost unheard of. People were buying out of the money put options—not totally unheard of, except these people were betting that Bear Stearns would drop by at least $45 a share in only a few days! With only a few days left until option expiration, people were buying massive amounts of extremely out-of-the-money put options in Bear Stearns.

Now this obviously makes you wonder why these people did this. What did they know? They knew *something* because Bear Stearns stock obviously collapsed with the JP Morgan bailout all over one weekend. You didn't have to have the information that these people had, just the knowledge of observing where the big money—the **smart money**—was doing. It would have required some research into the option market activity, and scanning the financial news websites for information regarding the volumes and monies going into this play with Bear Stearns. In addition, you could have picked up on the activity from reading *Investor's Business Daily* or the *Wall Street Journal*.

Add to this the fact that a massive amount of Bear Stearns's stock was being shorted. Bear Stearns reported 240 million total shares outstanding. Employees held approximately 72 million. Yet over 186 million shares traded on Friday, March 14—and to the downside! By accident, chance, or coincidence? We think not.

People do not make these kinds of bets in options and take such huge short positions without having some knowledge. What happened should never have been allowed to occur, but it did. The largest insider trading scam that no one ever heard anything about.

"Remember Friday, March 14, 2008," wrote Martin Wolf in the *Financial Times*. "It was the day the dream of global free-market capitalization died." If you had shorted the stock as the **smart money** did, you made a lot of money. A few thousand dollars invested in the out-of-the-money put options could have returned millions. This perhaps was the biggest insider trading scam in United States history—not only based upon the amount of money that was lost, but also by the fortunes made in such a short period of time that went totally unmentioned by the mass media and were not investigated by the SEC. Under normal situations, the SEC would have had its hands full investigating all of the insider trading that took place here. But they didn't. Why not? We can only surmise that someone (maybe the Federal Reserve) told the SEC to back off, and let this deal happen.

Remember that JP Morgan is part owner and founder of the Federal Reserve. The New York Fed advanced the funds for JP Morgan to buy Bear Stearns. Add the fact that Jamie Dimon, CEO of JP Morgan, sits on the board of the New York Fed and participated in the secret weekend negotiations. In fact, during the financial debacle that occurred in 2008, you did not read anything negative about the viability of JP Morgan. Imagine that. Surprise—*not!*

Unfortunately, this was an example of the biggest illegal insider trading scam perhaps in United States history. This should never have happened or been allowed to happen. Many people (judging by the record stock and option volume) profited from having this material non–public information that was clearly unethical and illegal to trade off of. How we could have made money ethically and legally would have been to follow where the *smart money* was being invested. This means that you would have had to observe the massive amounts of stock being shorted or you could have observed the unusual trading activity in the put options.

Remember that sometimes unforeseen events or acts of God can occur. If you want to increase your chances of making money, align yourselves with the *smart money*. Be on the right side for a change! We all know that the market is not here to make you money, but to take it.

What our government allowed to happen with Bear Stearns in particular is nothing short of tragic and incomprehensible. You can add Lehman Brothers to that as well.

As investors, we now know that the playing field hasn't always been fair. Wall Street was not proactive when it came to being transparent, honest, and compliant. Not only that, but the investment world has not been a level playing field for all of us for many years. We just didn't find out until it was too late and we lost money. If you are armed with this kind of information and knowledge, you too can become smart with your money—and significantly increase your net worth.

Remember that you don't necessarily want to do what everybody else is doing and/or thinking. The masses are like sheep and are easily led to the slaughter. And remember sheep get nervous and anxious when they hear noise. When it comes to investing, the masses get anxious and nervous when they hear noise or financial pornography.

You must think outside of the box and drink upstream from the herd. This is what being smart with your money is all about. It's more than just following the **smart money**; it's a philosophy that you can apply to all areas of your life.

Where to Find the Information

This is really easy if you are friends with or live next to Carl Icahn, a corporate insider, or an investment banker. If you're not, the next few paragraphs are really important to you.

The basic rule of thumb in trying to find out what really is going on requires you to look for sources that are not commonplace—and may not be well known to most investors. But today, we have the Internet, which is our gateway to information. And there is plenty of information available. The key is to find the credible, legitimate sources. In addition to independent news services, there are quite a number of independent newsletters published by credible people. These are by people whose number one objective is not to sell you a subscription but to have a higher purpose in conveying truth for the public good. Some of the websites that can be very useful to you in understanding the United States financial system would be www.fdrs.org and www.moneymasters.com. These two websites are very good to start with and we highly recommend that you spend some time on these to further educate yourself.

In order to find out where the big money and/or quiet money is going, you have to be willing to spend the necessary time to locate the information.

The key is to know where to look. Do not be frustrated if you don't find anything for days. We do not find good ideas every day or every week. But you will find them, and when you do, treat the information as if it is fresh hot bread. Use it while its fresh and you will be on your way to making money.

In order to track insider buys and sells, you can begin by simply going to Yahoo Finance. Once on the site, simply look up any stock quote and click on the "Insiders" tab for a list of the latest trades. Some insider filings may not appear in many databases until a month after the fact, but Yahoo seems to have one of the most current data feeds.

While we don't recommend that you use the SEC website, this is where the trading data is first sent. Once on the site, search for the central index key (CIK) for the company. The CIK is used on the SEC's computer systems to identify corporations and individuals who have filed disclosure with the SEC. Once you have the CIK, you can search for individual filings at: http://www.sec.gov/cgi-bin/srch-edgar.

In addition, *Investor's Business Daily* reports fund flows daily, and you can look to see where the big money is going. Stocks, bonds or funds that have greater than normal volume should also spark your interest, particularly in the absence of news. The *Wall Street Journal* and *Barron's* regularly feature small sections on insider purchases. You can also subscribe to websites that track insiders. We recommend www.insidercow.com and www.insidermonitor.com. These websites may or may not charge for their services, but the information you will receive is priceless and invaluable. You can also use www.recentinsider.com to find some excellent ideas. Avoid the publications written for the masses. You know what they are. They may be fine to read and have interesting articles, but not when it comes to finding where the *smart money* is.

Just as we are writing this book, Warren Buffett's Berkshire Hathaway was granted permission from the SEC to omit some information from its filings in order "to protect its trading strategy."[37] Imagine that. They don't want you and me to know what they are really doing. Unfortunately, they were granted their wish. Now, we believe that this is just a start of much more secrecy, non-disclosure, and hiding—whatever you want to call it.

Hedge funds love to try to disguise their trades and do not want the market (you and me) to know what they are doing. How do they do it? They may use a number of different trading firms to buy or sell a stock. In other words, they will piecemeal their orders. Instead of buying ten million shares at one firm, they may give the order to several different firms.

Take Peninsula hedge fund for example. If one had put money with Peninsula in 2000, you had a total gain of 1,236 percent in a little more than 10 years, according to Fortune magazine. How is that for return on investment? This is why it is so important to follow the **smart money**. Peninsula is **smart money**.

If you want to know the top holdings of these large hedge funds, consider looking for a report that Goldman Sachs publishes which consists of 50 stocks. Now, the largest hedge funds primarily consist of approximately 20 stocks give or take. They will also have exchange traded funds or ETF's in their mix. However, they are primarily used for hedging purposes, and not for investment purposes like what the mass media and Wall St. might portray to the masses to invest in.

---

37 Associated Press, Feb. 16, 2010

I know I am probably not pleasing many people by saying this, but it's more important that people understand what is really going on and realize that it isn't really a level playing field for us small investors. These guys set the rules because they are big money, quiet money, **smart money**. Just look at what Goldman Sachs went through testifying before Congress; they were recommending stuff to people while the firm took the exact opposite position. Do you really think that they are the only firm that does this?

This is why the futures game is so difficult for an investor to make money. When you take a position as an investor in the futures market, the firm has the right to take the exact opposite position. Who do you think is going to win that trade—an individual investor or a multibillion dollar firm? Exactly. In fact, it is clearly written on the new account form when you open a futures account that the firm has the right to take an opposite position. Sure there are exceptions when you have a major event that can move the market for you, but that is not the norm.

This is how the financial markets work and why you want to watch what they (the big boys, *the **smart money***) are doing. By the way, it's only going to get more difficult to obtain this information, particularly now that this book is out. Be aware—and get to work.

WHERE IS THE SMART MONEY TODAY?

Keep in mind that most of the information will probably be out of date by the time you read this. It is your job to ascertain where the **smart money** is and where the insiders are putting their own money.

In 2009, hedge funds and insiders made large bets on the banks during the financial crisis. You also saw big bets placed in commodities. In early 2010, hedge funds were shorting the S&P 500 and commodities. You knew not to invest in those sectors at that time.

When we talk about hedge funds, we pay particular attention to Paulson and Soros because both made a lot of money in 2008 and 2009, when others were getting killed. Most people have no clue why, but here is an example that explains it.

IndyMac Bank was closed and seized by the FDIC in July 2008. Okay, no big deal, you say. After all, there are many other banks whose assets were seized by the FDIC and sold off to another bank. In this particular case, the assets of IndyMac Bank were sold off to OneWest Bank in March 2009. Come to find out, the large shareholders of OneWest, a VP from Goldman Sachs, George Soros, and John Paulson. The sweetheart of a deal that these people have is absolutely amazing. We don't want to spend a lot of time explaining why it's important that these three people from OneWest Bank are making money, just how they are doing it. Basically, the FDIC covers 80–95 percent of all the mortgage loan losses, but the amount is calculated on the original loan balance, which means that the bank will make money off of each bad loan that they made! These guys will make money off of people like you and me (the taxpayers) paying for the bailout.

There are also a few other groups worth following such as Greenlight Capital, SAC Capital, Bridgewater Associates, JP Morgan, Harvard University, and Goldman Sachs. There are many others that are worth noting as well. Just do your homework.

The point that we are trying to make is that money moves. In fact, it is always moving. And at the time of this writing, the market is such that a buy-and-sell strategy is critical to preserving principal and making money.

In August and September 2011, we saw a large number of insider buys, like the Chairman and CEO of Hess Corp. (HESS) buying $10 million dollars of his own stock at around $58 a share. And in January 2012, he added another 91,250 shares at $54.79 for a total of $5 million dollars worth! What a great confirmation you have here, when the insider or CEO buys more shares!!!!!

This is the kind of information that you need to know whether or not you should be buying oil, like HESS. Based upon the information available, the answer is an unequivocal YES!

You also want to look at what the central banks are doing with their own money. As of October 2011, Korea and Thailand added more than $10 billion of gold to their reserves. Russia bought 5.95 tons. In fact, Russia has been steadily buying gold every month for the past five years, according to the IMF. Kazakhstan, Greece, Ukraine and Tajikistan have also been buying gold throughout the year. So, there is a bullish case for higher gold prices, because the central banks have been steadily buying. Add the fact that Soros bought a billion dollars of gold in the summer of 2012 through a gold ETF (GLD), and now you know what the **smart money** is doing with gold.

Look at Facebook (FB). Massive insider selling in the $37 range. Now, here at $19-$20, Donald Trump and George Soros have been buying along with other company insiders. Here is an example of a stock that **smart money** has been buying as of late.

Conclusion

We have tried to provide you with not only the philosophy that we utilize to decide where to put our money, but one that also can be used to understand politics, business, and other major events. Nothing political or economic happens by chance, coincidence, or luck. It is possible to not be like the masses and get slaughtered. But in order for this to happen, you must zig when others zag, think outside the box, and drink upstream from the herd. You will have to do your own research in order to find out what is really going on in the world. You must not believe the same way as the masses that are influenced so heavily by the mass media. Become connected to people who have accurate knowledge and information or utilize our strategies.

Now, I don't want you to think that following the **smart money** is just about tracking insiders, billionaires, and hedge fund managers. It is a way of investing that keeps you from following what is so heavily advertised and marketed to us. I am talking about mutual funds, fixed annuities, CD's. and Bonds. Remember you will never meet anybody who has made a fortune in fixed annuities, mutual funds, or bonds. Why? Because they don't exist.

You will find **smart money** in hedge funds and managed accounts whereby some sort of hedging or tactical asset allocation strategy is present. If you do not want to do the research that we have suggested that you do in this book, then find someone who does or find a good money manager or hedge fund manager. But do not put your money into bonds today, because you will pay above par for a high quality bond, with interest rates as low as they are. You don't necessarily want to buy fixed annuities today, because your money is not liquid, and interest rates are too low right now. And of course CD's don't pay anything as well. Other index annuities that you hear heavily advertised that provide you a bonus up front and guaranteed income for life should generally be avoided as well, unless you fully understand all the intricacies of these products and it represents only a small portion of your portfolio. Remember, you don't want to have to pay huge penalties to access your own money. It needs to be liquid and accessible at all times, not only because of the fact that there are many uncertainties and dramatic changes that can occur and will continue to occur in the future which will create opportunities to truly be smart with your money.

Know what the central banks around the world are doing in terms of interest rates and liquidity. Don't get the World Bank confused with the central banks. The World Bank lends money to foreign countries. The US holds veto power over major decisions that the Bank is involved in, and its president is appointed by the US president. The Bank has very little if any influence over the financial markets and consequently has no significance for us as investors.

Most importantly, pay attention to the Federal Reserve. They control the nation's money supply and exert more influence over our economy and financial markets than anything else (excluding our mass media, of course). Before you invest in anything, be aware of the general investing climate. If interest rates are low, and there is good liquidity in the financial system, then the stock market should do well. *Liquidity* is what really drives markets. Remember that they control liquidity by selling and/or buying Agencies (fixed-income securities from Fannie Mae or GNMA) and Treasuries. If you see the Federal Reserve buying Agencies or Treasuries in the open market, they are increasing liquidity. They do this through open market operations. Conversely, if the Fed is selling Agencies and Treasuries, then they are decreasing liquidity. If you watch what the Fed is doing and saying in regard to interest rates—and whether they are buying or selling paper—you will know what the market is going to do and you can invest accordingly.

> *The financial system has been turned over to the Federal Reserve Board. That Board administers the finance system by authority of a purely profiteering group. The system is private, conducted for the sole purpose of obtaining the greatest possible profits from the use of other people's money.*
> —Charles Lindbergh Sr. 1913

Before you buy any stock, you should know whether there are any insiders buying. If there are a number of insiders buying—and with big money—then that is your signal to seriously consider buying alongside them. Conversely, if you see insider selling, do not panic. Remember that people can sell for a variety of reasons. However, if you see massive insider selling by a number of insiders, be very cautious or simply avoid it. There are always other ideas with companies that do have insider buying in all types of markets.

If you don't want to go to the SEC website to look at each filing of every company every day, then simply subscribe to one of the websites that we mentioned. They do all the work for you and will provide you with the basic information that you need in order to find where the ***smart money*** is going. Sometimes it can be this simple.

Just keep in mind that high frequency trading has crept into our markets which has exacerbated the volatility in the markets. In fact, some say 70% of all daily trading volume is attributable to high frequency trading. Many are calling for the "short sale test tick rule" or SEC Rule 17 CFR 240.10a-1, most commonly known as the " uptick rule". This allows traders to execute short sales only if the previous trade caused an uptick in prices. The rule was created years ago to prevent the sort of cascading, snowballing selling that we see today. It was repealed on July 6, 2007.

Why the authorities allow this high frequency trading is beyond me. Obviously it is for a reason. They obviously want to increase market volatility to the downside.

Basically, this algorithmic trading is something similar to illegal front running. Co-location of mainframes with exchange computers, or having them in adjacent rooms is unfair to all of us because it gives them a head start over the rest of us. Much of the trading consists of these high frequency traders trading against each other placing deceptive orders. Orders that are large, sometimes out of the market orders with no intention of execution. If you or I were to do this kind of trading, we would be in jail.

Many people accuse the exchange authorities of an obvious conflict of interest by allowing members to reap huge custody fees from the high frequency traders, while the rest of us lose money.

Co-location fees are a significant revenue source per customer. This is all taking place, because the traditional revenue sources, like proprietary trading are disappearing thanks to Dodd – Frank. This is why in August of 2011, mutual fund redemptions were the highest in history. Investors were fleeing the market with all the crazy volatility. It just isn't an equal level playing field for all of us.

We are trying to level the playing field for everyone, and you can see what we are all up against. Just be aware that this exists and makes things even more difficult for us. This makes this **smart money** strategy and philosophy even more important, until the authorities enact some further legislation to help us individual investors.

This book can change your personal financial well-being and, more importantly, your life. This is my hope and purpose for writing this book. You should now understand the philosophy of big money and quiet money. You have seen examples of big money dating back hundreds of years and you have seen recent examples of the big money and the quiet money at work. You should also understand our definition of big money and how it relates to **smart money**.

The late, great, infamous investor, Sir John Templeton, stated, "It is impossible to produce superior performance unless you do something different from the majority." Here is one of the greatest investors substantiating why this philosophy works and is so important to successful investing.

Now you understand what **smart money** is—and how to find it and follow it. More importantly, you now know how the Fed and central banks operate and influence our financial markets.

Your minds have been opened and, armed with the know-how to truly follow the **smart money**, you know how to invest and make money. Now go be smart with your money!

It were not best that we should all think alike: it is the difference of opinion that makes horse races.
—*Mark Twain*

*Now you know how to think and invest with the **smart money**. Go and be smart with your money.*
—*Dr. B*

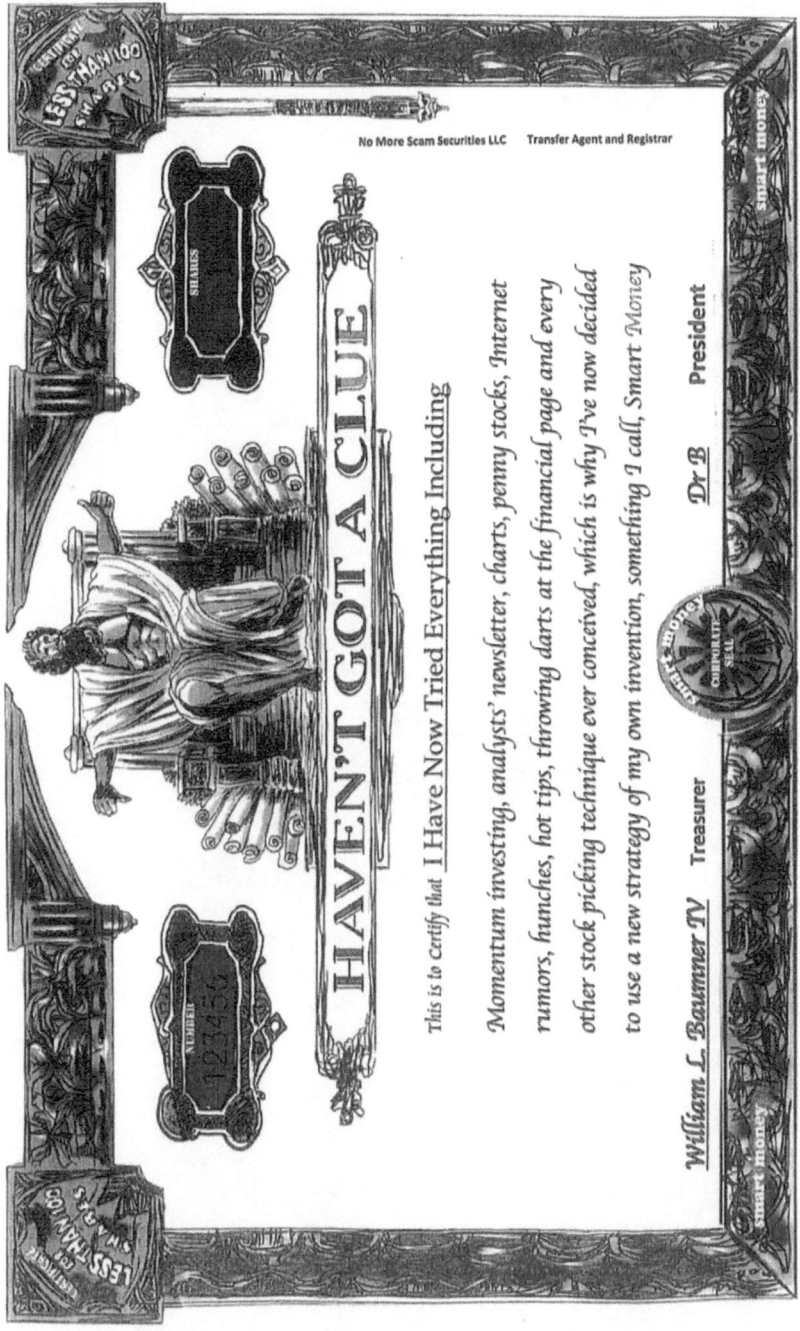

INDEX

A

Adelson, Sheldon 112
AIG 40, 67, 68
Aldrich Plan 55
American Airlines 116
American Pacific Corp 105
Apache 110
Associated Press 61, 63, 88, 125

B

Baker Hughes 110
Bank of America 32, 35, 68, 87, 105, 112
Barron's 84, 124
Bear Stearns 48, 56, 68, 72, 73, 119–122
Best Buy 111
Blinder, Alan 57
Bloomberg 71
Bridgewater Associates 128
Buffett, Warren 16, 106, 112, 113, 125
Burkle, Ronald 111

C

Capstead Mortgage 105
Central Bank 22, 30, 33, 36, 39, 41, 55, 57, 75, 76, 80, 82, 128, 129, 132, 135
Charles Schwab 90
CIA World Factbook 62
Citigroup 16, 67, 68, 106
Cohen, Steve 112
Congress 18–21, 34, 38, 40, 55–57, 67, 110, 126
Cramer, Jim 89

D

DeBeers 23
Dirks Test 93
DOW 10, 19, 59, 65, 89, 101, 113
Dr. B 136
DTCC 70
Dubai 62, 72, 112

E

Ellison, Larry 109
Enron 17, 95, 108

E-viaminvest.com 99

F

Fannie Mae 69, 133
FDIC 63, 127, 128
Fdrs.org 123
Federal Reserve 24, 27, 30–39, 40, 41, 51–53, 55–57, 75, 121, 132, 133
Felcor Lodging 108
Fidelity 1, 90
Financial Times 36, 120
Ford, Henry 38
Form 4 103, 104
Freddie Mac 69
Fuld, Richard 72

G

Garfield, James 53
Gates, Bill 90, 109, 112
General Electric 113
General Motors 111
Gold Inc. 105
Goldman Sachs 14, 17, 28, 44, 66, 70, 80, 82, 87, 95, 106, 114, 125, 126, 128
Goldseek.com 52
Goldwater, Barry 38
Greece 36, 129
Greenblatt, Joel 112
Greenspan, Alan 75
Gryphon Partners 70

H

Harvard University 128

I

Icahn, Carl 96, 112, 123
IndyMac Bank 127

J

Jefferson, Thomas 52, 57
Johnson & Johnson 114
JP Morgan 28, 33, 35, 40, 44, 48, 56, 67, 73, 74, 120, 121, 128

K

Kaufman, Ted 72
Kerkorian, Kirk 111, 112
Kirkland, Carl 107
Kudlow, Larry 89

L

Las Vegas Sands 105, 112
Lehman Brothers 12, 68, 71–73, 122
Los Angeles Times 67, 71
Lynch, Peter 1, 108

M

MBIA 107
McFadden, Louis 38
Merrill Lynch 87, 90, 116
Midway Games 111
Miller Exploration 110
Moneymasters.com 123
Morgan Stanley 116

O

OPEC 23, 26, 73
Options Clearinghouse 117
Owens, Robert 56

P

Paulson, John 112, 128
Pennzoil 110
Petroquest Energy 106

R

Redstone, Sumner 111, 112
Rockefeller, John 48
Rothschild, Nathan 54

S

SAC Capital 128
Salant, Richard 61
Seyhun, Nejat 100
Sheikh of Dubai 112
Short Selling 67–74, 114
Slim, Carlos 90, 112, 117
Smart Money iii, iv, viii, 3, 5, 6, 45, 65, 67, 79, 81, 83, 90, 93, 97, 106–108, 111, 112, 113–116, 125–128, 131–133, 135, 136
Soros, George 14, 112, 117, 128
South Dakota 69
Stock Market Crash 47, 48
Systemax 105

T

TD Ameritrade 90
Tennessee Coal 48
Thompson Financial 109
Trimbath, Suzanne 72
TrimTabs 109
Twain, Mark 136

U

Union Pacific 110
United Airlines 115
United Copper 48
Universal Express 70

V

ValueVision 107
Viacom 111

W

Warburg, James 64
Warburg, Paul 55
Washington Mutual 48, 56
Washington Post 71
Whole Foods 111
Wild Oats 111
Woodrow Wilson 57
Worth viii, 2, 6, 14, 19, 22, 42, 44, 48, 52, 53, 62, 73, 80, 84, 85, 94, 96, 97, 105, 113, 122, 128

Y

Yucaipa 111

www.ingramcontent.com/pod-product-compliance
Lightning Source LLC
Chambersburg PA
CBHW032342200526
45163CB00018BA/990